A Funny C

Other books by Des Sleightholme

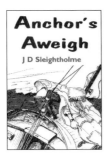

Anchor's Aweigh
ISBN 0 7136 4812 0
In his usual hilarious tongue-in-cheek manner, Des Sleightholme seeks to introduce the newcomer to the joys of cruising, explaining in a highly amusing manner how to go about choosing a boat, what is likely to happen on your first time out, coping with tides, knots and etiquette, and how to behave in marinas.

Off Watch with Old Harry
The funny side of sailing
ISBN 0 7136 4528 7
The 'joys' of antifouling, the bloody-mindedness of marine engines, the dubious pleasure of sailing on a spring tide, skippers lanunchings and novice crew are just some of the subjects aired by 'Old Harry'.

Old Harry's Dog Watch
ISBN 0 7136 4508 3
A highly entertaining collection of humorous observations which takes us through Des Sleightholme's many nautical hair-raising experiences

Up Aloft with Old Harry
IBN 0 7136 5040 0
Wickedly perceptive, Sleightholme attacks pomposity with scarifying gusto, taking the mickey out of everything and everybody afloat while covering such topics as leaking boats, dragging anchors, the charms of twin keels, the Fastnet Race, moving house by boat and, of course, the perils of going afloat.

DES SLEIGHTHOLME

A Funny Old Life

AN ANECDOTAL ROMP
THROUGH THE SAILING CAREER
OF DES SLEIGHTHOLME

Line illustrations by the author

Adlard Coles Nautical
LONDON

The cartoon on page i, by an unknown artist,
was displayed on *Yachting Monthly*'s stand at
the 1967 London Boat Show.

Published by Adlard Coles Nautical
an imprint of A & C Black Publishers Ltd
37 Soho Square, London W1D 3QZ
www.adlardcoles.com

First edition 2001
Reprinted 2003

ISBN 0 7136 5892 4

A CIP catalogue record for this book is available from the
British Library.

A & C Black uses paper produced with elemental chlorine-free pulp,
harvested from managed sustainable forests.

Typeset in 10½ on 12½pt Garamond Book
Printed and bound in Great Britain by
Cromwell Press, Trowbridge, Wilts

Foreword

I wish I could claim to have cut my teeth on a marline spike and that my father was an old Cape Horner with fingers missing and a taste for plug tobacco and navy rum, but I can't. I cut my teeth on a Farley's Rusk like everybody else, and father was a birdwatcher with a penchant for dandelion leaves who sang a lofty tenor in the choral society.

I never ran away to sea to watch 'the dawn come up like thunder' over Mandalay, and the salt in my blood was Epsom's. With generations of farmers in pork-pie hats in my wake, my natural aptitude for the nautical cock-up has been finely honed.

Never have I rounded Cape Horn backwards, crossed the Atlantic on a pedalo, won a race, or been pitch-poled in Force ten, but by heaven I know a thing or two about mud.

I left school at fourteen. The schoolmaster threw my exercise book at me one last time, like a benediction and said, 'I can't think what you're good for Sleightholme', implying that I might have some as yet undiscovered therapeutic value. He said he doubted that I would even make it as a road sweeper. Well that did it! I smacked my fist into my hand. By George I'd show 'em. I *would* be a road sweeper!

Sadly I never made it; I became a writer instead.

From infancy I have been motivated by the maxim 'If it floats *stand on it*'.

Des Sleightholme 2001

1

*A son o' the soil goes afloat for the first time
• Graduation from May Queen to
'Mixed Infants'*

Come to think of it our farm wasn't very efficient; our notions of husbandry were obsolete. There was grandad with string around his legs below the knee to discourage any mice that might be misguided enough to even think of venturing up his trousers, and there was father. Father lived with his old brass birdwatcher's binoculars screwed into his face, so he didn't see a hell of a lot that went on.

Father was a morning cold dip, raw carrot and deep-breathing freak. For a time he had a go at masticating his food forty times per mouthful; he also had a nervous sniff. What with his rotating jaws and sniffing, it was like watching a small steam engine at the breakfast table. 'Stop that Percy!' my mother used to say, and he did.

Grandad had one redeeming agricultural skill which held me

spellbound. He would be ploughing with me plodding along astern picking up worms – you could get huge worms that way. Suddenly he would rein in the horses. 'Whoa Prince, whoa Mettle!' Then he would whistle in a curious wheedling manner,

Me, sister and cousin Howard. He is the berk in the cap. He stuck a feather up my nose while playing red indians and locked me in the hen house. I was Big Chief Sucker.

1

whereupon the the horses would pee with great force and billowing clouds of steam. It didn't work when I tried; they just swung great hairy faces round and stared at me witheringly.

Our farmyard flooded in wintertime. What with cattle of every kind – for it was an Old MacDonald sort of farm – and a blocked drain or two, you'd get a substantial lagoon building up. The word has an exciting ring to it, 'lagoon', conjuring up visions of waving palms, coral sand and laughing Polynesians sporting in the surf. Well they wouldn't have wanted to sport in that little lot, mate! Their laughs would have snapped off a bit short, believe me. This was a yellowy brown, stinking blend of drainage, urine and liquid faeces. Having set the scene, along comes the infant Sleightholme, five years old and daft with it. It was 1925.

It was turning out to be a lousy day for me: our Godmother had come to tea. She wasn't your typical Godmother with wrinkled stockings and a loose denture who did the annual village hall panto 'good fairy' in a crêpe paper tutu. She was humourless but 'meant well' ... as they said about Nero. She came bearing gifts.

For my older sister, a great goofy doll with ringlets, removable knickers and rolling eyelids that made it look badly concussed. For me, a knobbly brown paper parcel that almost pulsated with promise. I ripped off the paper and found a little pair of shiny brown boots, for pity's sake! Brown boots with tabs bearing the legend 'Little Gents'. I let forth a great, booming howl and shot under the table.

Everyone was hugely embarrassed. Mother got a broom and swept me forth, bellowing. She forced me into those foul boots and sent me clattering out into the yard to 'play'. Which brings us back to that lagoon and an unforgettable experience.

Winter gales had unshipped a stable half-door which lay half in that foul liquid expanse. An idea took shape. It was probably one of my first, and it was certainly the worst. With an effort I launched it fully and then placed upon it one Little Gent followed by the other. For a brief, magical moment, a few golden seconds, I felt that unforgettable, that impossible sensation of buoyancy, of uplift, of a lateral gliding, a sense of destiny ... and then the bastard sank! It sank until the level of the filth reached the tops of my Little Gents and trickled coldly and horribly into my socks. For the second time that day my reverberating howls ripped apart the rural peace.

The early to mid-twenties was a time of agricultural and general depression. Bankruptcy haunted farmers. We kids were in bed one evening when my sister, knowing something was wrong, crept out onto the landing in her nightie and listened to our parents and grandad conferring. She heard mother say, 'In God's name what are we going to do?'

Poor little girl: ten years old and the whole world to sort out on her own. She crept back to bed and lay thinking and thinking while I, four years her junior, lay snorting and bumbling in untroubled sleep. It was as well that I didn't know my role on the morrow and how I was to be instrumental in attempting to restore the family fortunes.

Next morning she led me down the lane to the road and the bench upon which milk churns were placed for early collection. She had a basket which she proceeded to unpack. I watched, smirking. My smirk vanished. First came the old lace curtains, then the crown of daisies and a wand wrapped in silver paper. Finally she sat me on the bench holding a basin and wearing a card around my neck upon which was crayoned:

'MAY QUEEN please give genneressly.'

She might have given me a twisted id. I might have ended up liking handbags, you just don't know! I sat there for an hour feeling, for the first time in my life (although not the last), a total prat. Just one old man wobbled past on a bike. He gave me a very strange look.

None of which was furthering my nautical career. I had other character building experiences though, like the clip round the ear delivered by a miller. There was this windmill – an incredible thought today when the few working mills that survive mean heritage, tourism and school parties. I remember the clockity-whoosh of the great sails sweeping almost to the ground and how I jumped up to touch one. Clunk, round the earhole. Let's call it a history lesson. I sure as hell remember the sound of windmills.

Then there was the 'dilly cart'. That was what they called it: a low-slung cart, a metal tank on spindly wheels used to carry excrement or 'night soil', as it was euphemistically known. It was boat-shaped. We all had earth closets: holes in the ground topped by a seat with holes of varying sizes to suit posteriors of greater or lesser area. At long intervals came the dilly man with his cart and a bucket on a pole to empty the hole. The contents were his perk and would be spread on his smallholding to raise tomatoes of prodigious size and colour.

Mother took us to tea at the dilly man's place. 'Go out to play,' she said, unwisely in view of the last time when I'd found the stable door. My sister went off, messing around with the hens. But the wheels of the float were designed for five and a half year old boys to climb, best shorts and pullover or not. There was about six inches of filth in the bottom and my Little Gents drew about four and a half.

The inevitable farm sale was pure Victorian eat-your-heart-out drama, and I learned the meaning of sheer misery. Father, defeated in the trade of his forebears, was to go back on his tools as a general engineer. This meant selling up and moving to Yorkshire: a fresh start. The agents had instructions to send our furniture on ahead and flog off the tat, but some cloth-eared muffin got it wrong!

Indoor stuff outside in the yard looking sad and grubby. People, men in leather gaiters, poking with sticks. Our old farm dog Ben was tied to a cart looking bewildered and frightened. He saw me and his tail wagged frantically with relief. He licked my hand, then I was dragged away. The look in Ben's old eyes still haunts me over seventy years later: 'Why? What have I done?' I learned about treachery from poor old Ben.

Childhood raced by with crisis-to-crisis carpeting – from our arrival at our new home to the spoutless kettle, the broken bedsteads and grandad having one of his funny turns. It was right up to standard.

I started school, a Catholic Primary, and found myself a mixed infant. Our education was administered by three nuns, which sounds like a pipe tobacco. They were the Sisters Everilda, Agnes and Finnian, which sounds like a close harmony trio. This was far from the truth: the Finnian was olde-tyme bog-Irish, hard as a shillelagh, harder of eye and wielding a yet harder cane.

I was to leave that school six years later, academically almost a virgin, but my recital of the Apostles' Creed at various speeds and in various voices excited a great deal of comment at the time.

2

Afloat twice • The secrets of the confessional • Girls shouldn't climb creepers • If it floats sit on it

The urge to float on things is fundamental to mankind, from the ancients on their logs, or tribesmen on mussucks (inflated goatskins) like hairy bagpipes, to the super-tanker and the holiday-maker making nice time off Beachy Head on his Lilo. Being stuck in the middle of Yorkshire cramps your style.

Water drew me like a magnet, sometimes with regrettable results. On Bank Holidays and Catholic Holidays of Obligation ('obligation' being the key word since there was no chance of ducking out) there were family cycle rides and picnics. We took in Fountains Abbey, The Devil's Arrows, the moors and various waterfalls.

I was the only one without a bike. I rode on father's crossbar. He'd fitted a little wooden saddle, 'padded' with a bit of old carpet. There were stirrups. It was bloody uncomfortable. Half an hour of that and I was squirming around like a lap dancer. 'Keep still, keep STILL!' father would howl, wobbling all over the road. On arrival I would dismount and lurch around bandy-legged like six-gun Pete.

We came to a bridge with people leaning over, staring down, so we stopped and joined them. Men were dragging a drowned sheep out of the water, an event which, in those placid times, was one worthy of study. It was then that I disgraced myself, let down the whole family and left mother 'not knowing where to put her face', implying that it was portable and hard to stow.

There was a lady in a tweed pork pie, with a brick red face, who spoke with what mother called a refined accent. So she switched on her own version, ordinarily reserved for doctors and Father O'Brian. It was a back-of-the-nose ventriloquist voice (ay ged gat givout gooving gy gips). They were hooting away at each other, but I had to chip in! Enunciating clearly and loudly for the benefit of all, I said, 'You can see it's a female sheep *because it's got tits.*' There was a very long silence.

We mounted, me with ears aflame and deep, deep in the gravy. I had ruined the day. Mother had never been so ashamed; where had I heard 'that word'? For my own part I felt cruelly wronged. I knew a tit when I saw one, even at six.

There was another outing though, which proved to be exciting beyond all expectation and which fuelled my longing to get afloat to fever pitch. Now there was a cushion lashed to my saddle, diminishing the risk of my becoming a castrati doomed to trill my life away in some monastery, but it was still wickedly uncomfortable.

We picnicked in a wooded dell barred with sunlight and with water at the bottom cleaving a jungle of huge wild rhubarb and scarlet willow-herb – an English wood before the chemists got at it. The air was a somnolent hum of every sort of insect: plain, coloured and striped. Lazy butterflies drifted, and huge, impractical, home-made-looking dragonflies rustled by. A kingfisher did a streak like a blue bullet, woodpeckers tock-tocked, and from holes in the bank of the river whiskery faces peered critically.

I remember we had bottled lemonade instead of the stuff mother made up from vivid yellow crystals; this was fizzy and no good to us. Father said so. 'That muck's no good for them!' he stated, setting the seal of its desirability once and for all. Then we heard the drum.

From around the bend it came, chum, chum, chum, like that. And above the foliage rose puffs of blue smoke. There was a sudden movement of the water; coots skittered squawking. And then the barge appeared. It was rolling back a tumble of bow-wave, and looked enormous, breathtaking, trailing a wake which broke hissing among the reeds, smacking and sucking in holes and crannies. I just stood and gaped.

The barge drew abreast. Yellow, red, blue she was painted with a black funnel that puffed smoke rings. There was a figure at her tiller, the luckiest man in the world – except that it was a woman. She was wearing a cloth cap and smoking a pipe. I waved and she waved back.

When father's firm went bust he ended up on the dole. We became permanently broke, and I learned about humiliation. Mother in the grocers, fumbling in her purse for money she knew wasn't there ... 'Oh dear, will you put it on my account please?' Only she no longer had one.

'Perhaps you'd better put a few items back, Mrs Sleightholme.'

Toes curled up in shoes, but the floor didn't oblige me by opening up.

She gave piano lessons to tone-deaf little morons who didn't want to be there in the first place; it was like making bricks with sand. A sock making machine was bought with ill-spared capital. 'Make ££££'s at home in your spare time, we buy all you make ... pleasant, easy and profitable work.'

Had there been a market for woollen fire hose we would have been quids in, but *mother couldn't turn the heel!* It chattered and gnashed while she wound away at the handle. Father came in for some stick, he being an engineer yet unable to fathom it out. Grandad kept quiet. It consumed a king's ransom in wool before being stuffed in the attic.

L odgers came next. More accurately, foreign students who wished to live *en pension* while polishing up their English. They spent three months with us and returned home fluent in broad Yorkshire dales dialect. One of these was Monet from Nice, sixteen years old, olive complexioned and incandescent with burgeoning sexuality.

She was also a tomboy who climbed the ivy with a lavish display of knicker. She climbed the ivy quite a lot; I got to know her knickers better than she did. We had the Territorials camping nearby. They hung around our house like redskins circling a covered waggon. There was this sergeant in particular. Mother told father to have a word with him and he had two: one was 'er' and the other was 'um'. So she did it. His stripes wilted. He curled up like a salted slug and, to my dismay, Monet was sent home, and I was left suffering from knicker starvation.

On Saturday nights we all went to confession. 'Pray father, I have had mucky thoughts ten times!'

Nobody knew that my prayerbook had a section at the back dedicated to the examination of conscience. It listed every sin this side of hell with Capital Sins asterisked like the dish of the day; take your pick, shop around. The priest in his wheelhouse was bog-Irish like the Finnian. 'Mother o' mercy ye've never done dem tinks, never at all, at all!', he groaned. 'Away widgee and say an Our Farter and tree hail Marys.'

Then I got afloat properly for the second time in my life.

The River Ure was sourced in the dales and given to flash flooding, dangerous because it could rise ten feet in two hours which made it irresistible to boys. There was an area called the Willow Garth where the river spread wide and shallow with jungly banks and midstream islands of shingle around which the rattling, prattling, tinkling, rustling waters divided. Sunlight made a diamond cascade of glitter as painful to the eye as a welder's torch. As you waded thigh-deep from island to island a sunken branch nodded rhythmically. Trout darted. Crayfish trundled.

During school holidays this magical place lured us. We fished for minnows, crouching on the grassy bank. There was catmint and the garlic scent of wild ramson. Nowadays I can sniff it in the garden and go spiralling back down the vortex of time to become ten again with scabby knees and hair slicked down with spit. You could peel willow bark to make a whistle, and blow vulgar raspberry noises.

But then, downstream, black and dangerous, there was 'The Hole'. 'You're not to go near The Hole', people told you, enhancing its attraction as a place not to be missed.

Illness in early infancy had left me a bit frail. 'Let the lad run wild', the doctor had advised, steepling his fingers, drumming up potential future business. The Hole, as a recuperative measure, promised the ultimate cure.

Neither could I swim, despite school visits (whenever the weather was dull and chilly enough) to The Bathing Station. There was this sour bastard in a cloth cap called The Instructor. He had a pole from the end of which dangled a rope and a stout canvas belt. His method was basic: the child descended wooden steps into the black chill of chest-deep water and bent over, supported by the belt. 'Wun-two, wun-two, wun-two', he would chant while the child lashed the water to foam in a desperate parody of the breaststroke. At intervals, by way of testing, the old swine dunked the luckless student, then hoisted the sufferer gasping and spluttering. We hated swimming lessons.

The Hole was downstream of the shallows where the river narrowed. Gone were the merry little ripples and the chatter and sparkle. Suddenly the river fell silent and slid swiftly into blackness where swirls and tiny whirlpools darted about the sleekie surface. It was utterly evil.

I was with Four-eyes, my current mate at the time. He had given me a thumping, but we remained firm friends. There was a boy lore that said you couldn't hit a lad who was wearing glasses – Four-eyes kept his on so I couldn't hit him back. His dad was an angler.

'Dad says there was an aud party drowned in't 'ole' Four-eyes said. 'Er 'air was full of srimps, all 'oppin!' He gave a graphic impersonation of a corpse rolling its eyes and flopping about. Also, according to Four-eyes' dad, there was a gigantic pike lurking there. It was one hundred years old and had once snatched a child off the river bank. It could have snatched Four-eyes and done everybody a good turn.

Winter floods had left a large log wedged among the willows. It was banana-shaped and would just support your weight. It taught us to swim. We took turns in floating down through the shallows and towing it back upstream for another go. I was aboard, floating, with Four-eyes shoving from behind. We should have stopped before we reached the deep part. That lousy little swine *shoved with all his strength.* Suddenly there was blackness below me.

It took forever to drift down over The Hole while Four-eyes kept pace hollering a commentary like a coach courier. 'Yer just comin' to where't police pulled that old tart out ... it was about 'ere where't pike got 't nipper.' My legs felt ten feet long. I clung on. I'd kill him. When finally I reached the next shallows; only one thing saved Four-eyes from my terrible wrath: *I had been on a voyage.*

9

3

*I see the sea • Become leader of the
Woodpecker Patrol • Bring on one of
Mother's Bad Heads*

Money was desperately tight. Mother went around looking defiant, and I felt guiltily ashamed of her. She was wearing odd-looking cast-offs she'd been given and had hoped to disguise by altering. She was a lousy seamstress. There was a dreadful suit that she made for me when I had to be page boy to the church May Queen (there's a sour coincidence if you like!). It was pale green, shiny, and the shoulders puffed up sideways. A boy said I looked a proper little ponce ... I thought he said prince.

Mother's savings gave us a day excursion to the seaside. It was a pre-dawn start with mother making sulphureous egg sand-

Pageboy in the fearful suit mother made. Jealous contemporaries said I looked a proper little ponce. Any fool knows you spell 'prince' with an 'i'. My father developed his own photos behind a blanket under the stairs; they faded like the Cheshire cat's grin.

10

Beach-wear circa 1927. Father is wearing the bathing pants that mother knitted. When wet they sagged and stretched. He looked like a Turkish peasant and had to swim one-handed. 'Don't throw the beach-ball to your father, Desmond!'

wiches and filling Thermos flasks. We went to Redcar. My sister and I were frantic with excitement which meant that we sat po-faced watching the countryside swoop by wreathed in engine smoke.

My first, my very first glimpse of the sea took me by surprise. Fields and woods fell away, and there was a straight line across the sky. Above it there were grey clouds, below it grey nothing. Father said, 'Look, the sea!' in a proprietorial manner, as if he'd just made it.

The tide was out, and the North Sea was visible as an angry white scar beyond a seemingly limitless expanse of sand. A bleak and shrivelling blast of wind blew. We had our towels and cossies. It was like some solemn rite – The Dip.

Grandad was absent; he'd elected to stay home. In line abreast, clad in our stripie bumble-bee swimming costumes, we slapped seawards. As the water reached our ankles, then, by infinitely slow degrees via puddles and deepening pools, our knees. Father became strangely skittish. The wind came non-stop from Bear Island. Father flung himself forward; he shrieked like a wounded animal. 'Come on, it's lovely!' he sobbed in a tortured falsetto ...

The notorious Means Test rule deemed that owning a piano constituted a luxury inconsistent to being on the dole. Grandad got asthma, the Hunger Marchers trudged through town, mother scalded herself from head to foot and wouldn't get a doctor in case it cost too much, and it was a wet summer. Despite this, *somehow*, she bought me a scout uniform.

I took to scouting the way converts find salvation. The khaki shirt itched like some form of penance, but I was tufted with bits of ribbon, spattered with badges, and I had a woggle and a sheath knife which nowadays would get you arrested on the spot. I had a whistle, a pole, a coil of rope on my hip, and, glory of glories, I had a huge floppy hat. At the age of eleven I appeared to be walking on stilts – my limbs were so endless and knobbly like bamboo furniture that you could have stood a pot plant on my head. In group photos my head was always out of the frame but my knees came out a treat. We'd have sing-songs which in broad Yorkshire defied transcription: 'We're all down in't cellaroil wher't muck clarts on'twinders'. Another one was about a graveyard: 'T'worms crawl in an't worms crawl out, in by tha gob and out by tha snout.' Heady stuff, by George!

Leader of Woodpecker patrol in full plumage, hat, whistle and woggle. Note the position of the knife; sudden bending threatened instant emasculation. No other scout had a bent staff (which usually means fiddling the petty cash): psychiatrists note.

My promotion was rapid. In no time at all I was made patrol leader of the Green Woodpeckers, how about that? Each patrol had its distinctive call according to its adoptive creature; thus we barked, cooed, pee-witted, and chattered imitatively. My call was one that called for practice. One evening, after a meeting, I was loping homeward through the dusky lanes, my ribbons flopping, accoutrements jangling. I decided to practise the cry of the Green Woodpecker or Yaffle. 'Keckkekkekkekkek!' I screeched, jerking my head back and forth typically and flapping my elbows. And there she was, this bloody woman leaning over her gate. She recoiled as if stung. She twisted around. 'Harry!' she hollered. 'Coom an' look at this daft bugger!'

My quest to get afloat received a shot in the arm: father took us on the river. It was a special treat. There was a boating station with rows of skiffs moored like bunches of fruit, each with a cushioned seat in the stern and a backrest emblazoned with a name. We had *Cynthia* in peeling gold paint. There was a rudder and steering lines. A man in waders asked father, 'As ter rowed a boat afore, mister?' 'Yes,' father said, lying through his teeth.

To my disgust the man addressed me as 'sonny'. I sat aft with sister who showed her bloomers, and mother who was showing a lot of stocking top which he eyed appreciatively. Mother steered about as efficiently as father rowed. Oar blades circling and splashing, boat zigging and zagging, we moved upstream until a bend hid us from view. The man in the waders was shading his eyes in a would-you-bloody-credit-it sort of way and my shame was utter.

It was half an hour of, 'Keep still ... watch the bank Percy ... DON'T MOVE.' We returned with our bows festooned with foliage, but we had been afloat, water had smacked and slapped our bows, we had rocked and dipped and gone hissing into reeds, we had been splashed and the oars had click-clocked in rowlocks. If only, though, if only I could have had a go at rowing!

The adults in my life furthered my maritime ambitions the way bandy legs benefit Olympic hurdlers. I was twelve and looking around.

Father was gentle, totally unassertive, defeated by misfortune, an outdoor man condemned to the indoors, and a loner in a crowd. He lived for birds, wild flowers, singing tenor and health food. Ergo the red face, the nervous sniff and the penchant for immersion in freezing water.

Mother was vibrant, ebullient, artistic, assertive, immensely emotional and a natural leader. She worked for us, thought for us, decided everything for us (because somebody had to) and ruled by emotional blackmail. 'Oh Desmond,' she'd say, 'you'll bring on one of my bad heads!' I would visualize one of those huge carnival heads and her with a bad one.

4

Some rum buggers in 'Ull • 'Come in number nine!' • The nomad years • You could row 'er on a dewy lawn • The thirty-bob syndicate

Father, digging holes for telegraph poles, odd-jobbing, queuing for his dole, munching his dandelions, needed organising. Mother began job-searching for him. She wrote him some glowing references – footnoted to the effect that 'Originals were available on request', knowing full well that people are inherently lazy and would never take up the offer. In 1932 she landed him a job at a bus depot in Hull. It was a stratagem she was to use repeatedly in future years.

Father had a fresh air fetish and a loathing for artificial light which compelled him to switch off lights and fling open windows, thereby plunging every workshop into a gloom pierced by a howling gale. Workmates who valued a brightly lit fug and protested en masse had him sacked ('It's 'im or us boss!') almost as fast as mother could write job applications. But he lasted two or three years in Hull.

The city was huge, an urban sprawl unlike anything I had every known. People were different kids knew more about everything. At school my age group were into things like algebra; *I had never even heard of it!* They were halfway through the second textbook.

A man came knocking on our door, and mother opened it expectantly. He was ordinary-looking but with a mad eye. He leaned forward confidentially. 'Shhhh', he said, finger to lips, about to reveal a secret. Mother leaned forward to listen.

'There are some rum buggers in 'Ull missus!' he said. And with that he left. The incident delighted her and me too. You remember little things such as that; they affect you profoundly. They are the psychological gravy stains that nothing can shift. I was going to enjoy Hull. On foggy nights I could lie in bed and hear the ships' sirens out on the river. They were eerie, haunting, immensely moving, and I would fight off sleep to listen to them.

Hull City was presided over by a statue of William Wilberforce which stood on a tall pillar. It gave great joy to small boys on rainy days. The sculptor had given the figure a rolled scroll to hold ... at a most unfortunate position and angle. It collected and projected rainwater outwards and downwards, creating the happy illusion that the great man was peeing down on the world with force and accuracy. Mentioned in no guide book, this spectacle was one of the famous sights of the City.

A tuppenny tram-ride took me to the fish-docks where the battered, rusty, turtle-decked Icelandic trawlers jammed the kipper-reeking basins along with oil, dead cats and fish guts. It was a magical place and rich with opportunity for a lad in search of death or mutilation. Shunting engines hissed and clanged, and men rushed around dragging coils of wire trawl-gear. Barrows, pushed at break-neck speed by yelling dockies, hurtled around corners. It was vibrant and colourful, the Real Thing, ... 'Booger off outer it son!' bawled a dockie authentically. A dock policeman gave me the bum's rush back out of the main gates.

School was a nightmare. I was so far behind, particularly in maths, that I was hailed the resident idiot, a failure to be paraded by teachers as an example to others. I dreaded, loathed and detested school and consequently adopted the role of prize moron. I was good on roller skates and at whittling wood – which I could do simultaneously at grave risk of self-disembowelment.

I lived for Saturday mornings when Mother gave me my weekly sixpence and I could skate to the public park. My skates were the cheapest that money could buy and would bend in the middle when I hit bumps, so there were frequent stops to bash them straight. Other kids had ball-bearing, self-steering skates, and I hated their living guts.

Once at the park the boating lake was my goal. There was a fleet of pram dinghies as well as skiffs. It was a far cry from father and his windmilling oarsmanship and from being compelled to sit bolt upright to preserve equilibrium. Nowhere was the boating lake more than three feet deep and so there were no safety strictures in force. For threepence you got half an hour. I always asked for boat number nine.

Every Saturday I'd be there, in heaven. There was an ornamental island in the middle of the lake, its planked edges indented like a pie-crust by the scars of countless stunning crashes. Here a group of ornamental waterfowl with scarlet and scandalised faces huddled protectively together under a meagre willow. Once I was over the

15

initial stage of rowing in narrow circles and colliding with other rotating beginners I began to row flat out. I learned to round up alongside the landing stage with panache and a swirl of water. The boatman wore crutch-high waders to enable him to stride mightily to the rescue of lesser oarsmen, and a peaked cap as if to emphasise his importance and nautical status. 'Nonner that, nonner that!' he'd admonish. 'Tha'll stove't bloody bows in, boy!'

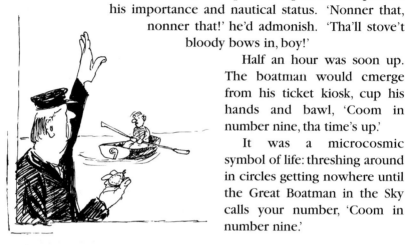

Half an hour was soon up. The boatman would emerge from his ticket kiosk, cup his hands and bawl, 'Coom in number nine, tha time's up.'

It was a microcosmic symbol of life: threshing around in circles getting nowhere until the Great Boatman in the Sky calls your number, 'Coom in number nine.'

We lived on a housing estate, each house with its back garden plot and a wireless pole. Radio Luxembourg on Sunday mornings after mass. I was one of the local gang of delinquents. *Boy's Own Paper* provided lethal advice for 'Young Chemists' on how to make carbide volcanos and manufacture gunpowder: you drilled a hole in the top of a post, filled it with home-made gunpowder and, with a hammer lashed to a pole, whacked a six inch nail down until it exploded. We did the gateposts of anybody we didn't like. We also learned how to jam radios.

'Solly' Solomon had a young electrician's kit. There was this ex-copper who hated kids and liked listening to fights on his radio. We'd set up our equipment at the foot of his pole in the dark, and we'd watch his shadow on the curtains bounding around, thumping his wireless and cursing.

But it wasn't all boys ... there was Betty. In all innocence I tried to teach her scouting, for pete's sake! The Art of Natural Camouflage, which meant squirming around in the long grass; girls are useless at that sort of thing. She said, 'If you was to lie on top of me, nobody would even know I was there.' Would you believe it?

The banks of the river Humber at Hessel were ideal for camping, being fringed by saltings and infested with every creature that crawled and bit. Dekko and I loaded our trolleys and set off for a scouting weekend. The tide was high; barges and a coaster passed. 'We'll swim', Dekko said. We never got deeper than our knees which was where the mud reached. Then we had to wipe the mud off with grass which was alive with sandhoppers.

Two little girls appeared and began jeering and betting we couldn't catch them. How absurd can girls get? They ran off squealing and, of course, we caught them no bother at all. Mine offered to show me something I'd never seen before, I mean *me*! At twelve years old! Dekko was gone a long time so I went to look for him. When we got back to our camp some swine had stolen our sausages!

We awoke next morning to bright sunlight wondering what the hell time it was, not having watches. We were as stiff as alabaster bishops in a church. I said, 'It's got to be eight o'clock.' 'Easy,' Dekko said. It was time for a sausage-free breakfast, and he offered to go get some water to make tea. There was a cottage close by.

Dekko had to bang hard and repeatedly on the door before he got any response, then a bedroom window shot up and a man's tousled head was stuck out. 'What the bloody hell do you want?' he snarled.

'Please mister can you let me have some water?' Dekko asked nicely.

The man appeared to be having breathing difficulty; maybe it was asthma. 'Yes,' he said. 'Yes by God. I'll let you have some water!' In those days few cottages had bathrooms what they had was a big basin and jug of water.

Dekko came back with an empty can, soaked and cursing. 'That bleeder says it's only half past four!'

Father was a very cautious man. If he'd taken up yogic flying he'd have worn a parachute. He couldn't drive and wouldn't learn, which can impede your career plan in a bus depot. Mother started writing references again ... with an atlas at her side. She was passionate about history and Pontefract, 'which means a broken bridge,' she explained. She landed him a job in a bottle factory.

It was back to middle England and curly kale country. No ships' sirens groaned on foggy nights, and my maritime longings languished. I had little to offer the world of work. I left school at

R.S.P.C.A. (Ripon Branch).
PET SHOW, 1931.
Thomas Guinea Pig, Agosto v 9
THIRD PRIZE
Desmond Lloyd

*My credentials: the only certificate I ever won apart from one
for swimming fifty yards on back and front. Thomas was a
liver-and-white guinea pig with a hint of mange. Without that
I might have come FIRST, then Lord knows what heights I
might have reached!*

fourteen with one certificate: Third Prize for a brown and white
guinea pig called Thomas. There had been four entries, and one of
them had mange.

So no grammar school, no university, and no job sweeping roads
because we never stayed around long enough. In a couple of years
we moved five times. Father would go ahead and find digs, and we'd
follow once he'd found a house to rent – usually a decaying
Edwardian semi reeking of gas leaks and cats.

The moves were inspired either by his job dissatisfaction, his
boss's dissatisfaction, or because his shuddering workmates said it
was either him or them. One time we arrived in the removal van to
be met by father with his toolbox, a sure sign he'd just been given
the boot.

From Pontefract to Yeovil in Somerset (Avalon and King Arthur),
to Barnstable in north Devon (Exmoor and Lorna Doone), to
Heathfield near Newton Abbot (Dartmoor and hut circles), to the
Isle of Wight (Carisbrook Castle). Along the way we lost father's
fossils, acquired a lurcher named Paddy who bit, and father ate the
spider. This episode came about from his habit of munching his
health cereal in total darkness. The spider felt gritty and was bloody

enormous. It started him off doing eye exercises, rolling his eyeballs in an eerie fashion and swivelling them up, down and sideways. Mother said, 'Stop that Percy!' He stopped.

On the Isle of Wight I met Spoofer Murray. Spoofer was younger than me in years but, older in artifice. He lived with his grandad and mum and, like me, had been sickly as an infant. His mum had also been up all night with his chest, implying some form of Bacchanalian revelry and excesses with Vick Vapour Rub. You knew when he was lying because his voice went up in pitch and his brow furrowed. He was always in deep gravy.

He found the silver spoons wrapped in newspaper in a drawer, obviously superfluous and unlikely to be missed. The pawnbroker, a father himself and no stranger to perfidy, stuck tongue in cheek. 'I'll have to see if they're worth anything; leave your name and address, son.' Which the muffin did. In today's terms grandad 'abused his Human Rights', wielding a vengeful slipper.

One day Spoofer appeared waving a sword; it was shiny and looked, and was, razor sharp. 'Grandad threw it out', he said. It turned out to be the Malay Kris that hung in a scabbard on the dining room wall, and it was grandad's after dinner talking point. He had been in the Malaysian Police, and this Malay went amok, heads flying like bean-bags. 'I drew my pistol and he came at me with *this!*' grandad would cry with drama, whipping it out of its scabbard. There was no blade. The handle was pegged in with a bit of firewood. Spoofer didn't come out for over a week.

We had Wootton Creek but no boat. We agreed that this was intolerable. There were always hulks rotting on the saltings. What you did was waggle the transom ... if the stem remained unmoving the boat was usually beyond hope. The boats subjected to this rigorous test failed dismally but there were boats for sale, advertised on postcards in the paper shop.

There was *Mickey Mouse*, home-made in plywood, ominously coffin shaped, high-sided and narrow. To keep her upright she had a keel with a length of heavy gas pipe bolted on. She would have sunk like a diving gannet. Then there was Les Warman's flattie, fifteen bob with paddles. 'That boat would do you nice', said Les. 'Why you could row'n on a dewy lawn, son!' which was a sensible suggestion seeing that there were gaps in her planks you could have posted a letter through.

Me at the helm and Spoof on jib sheets in a borrowed boat on Wootton Creek. We were inseparable, like jam tart and trouser seat.

'Read that!' Spoofer told me one day. An ad in the local paper. It read 'Ten quid complete, 16ft clnkr fully rigged all gear new apply Sunbeam Yard.' I said, 'Don't be bloody silly, we don't have that sort of money!' He had a plan.

A man in an apron, powdery with sawdust which stuck to his moustache, showed us the boat. She was in a shed and looked huge. He whipped off a cover. We saw the chestnut gleam of her hull, pale golden spars, gleam of oar-blade and coiled buttermilk newness of ropes. We made him turn everything out for our inspection, including the sails which were so new that the sail maker's pencil

20

strike-up marks still showed. My heart was heavy with foreboding. Spoofer had a plan?

'To business,' Spoofer said, businesslike. 'Tell you what we'll do. Ten quid right? Well, we'll give you twelve quid. Shilling a week, two bikes and an airgun!'

The man appeared to be thinking deeply; he was taking deep and beneficial gulps of air. Then he spoke, and his voice had a curious tremor. 'Now I'll tell you what *I'll do*,' he said. 'I'll give you young buggers a count of ten, then gawd help yer!'

Then I had my first sail. Spoofer's grandpa had a boat. He was a dapper military man: shaved red-raw, toothbrush moustache, shiny-shoe immaculate. So was his boat. Spoofer said, 'Don't go mate, or at any rate don't say I never warned you!' I ignored him.

Grandpa arrived at the shore clad in reefer, cream slacks and a big cap like a soufflé. I rowed out, showing off my skills. I swirled alongside. He said, 'Boat oars blades forr'd man. This isn't some damn bum-boat!'

The boat was a fourteen foot half-decker with sparkling paint and brightwork. There was a speck of seaweed ... he tut-tutted and messed around getting it off with a fingernail.

There was a cover with dozens of ties, then a sail coat and more ties. There were innumerable little lockers and, in each, just one item: shammy leather, dustpan, scrubber, and so on. I got the gaff mainsail up unaided, having read exhaustively on the subject.

'Peak up and wrinkle your nock man!' grandpa said indignantly, making no concessions for my state of sailing virginity. 'Sweat up, belay and toggle your fall!'

God, it was terrific, the real thing: me, sailing at last! It was all so new yet familiar. We were out for two hours. We hove-to and munched our sandwiches off Ryde Pier, and hooted at by the ferry. Later he simply handed over the helm to me so that he could pee in the bailer, which he held exactly square throughout. I luffed her. He howled imprecations so I bore off and got another earful. I was sick. Heinz Vegetable Salad sandwiches. It looked the same before and after consumption. 'Chin off the side-deck man, chin off the side-deck!' he snapped.

I got home in a trance. 'I've been rucking my nock,' I told mother. She said, lowering her voice, 'You were right to tell mother, Desmond. Remember, there is *nothing* that you can't tell mother!'

Spoofer was still at school. He had a colleague called Rick whose dad was a crabber at Bembridge and had a fourteen foot pot boat for sale for thirty bob. It was a vast sum but we had a syndicate of three, and we could at least make an offer. We pedalled off to see him.

We looked at the boat first and gave her the waggle test. 'God!' Spoofer said. 'She's as good as new!' She had two foot of good-as-new bilge water in her, crabs' legs and an assortment of fish guts, and odd oars.

The door opened to reveal a woman with a mouth full of clothes pegs, surrounded by billows of steam like a pantomime genie. 'Father!' she bawled over her shoulder. We followed her in. It was a matto grosso of suspended washing through which we fought our way. Rickie's dad was bent over a wireless set listening to a race commentary. He held up a hand. The commentary rose to its climax and ended. 'Sod it!' he said, then to us, 'What then?'

It was a simple transaction. We offered twenty-five bob. 'Thirty or piss off,' he said. We handed it over and became boat owners.

O ur syndicate consisted of me, Spoofer and 'Dinger' Bell, and ten bob each. Paul came in later with a two quid outboard, a cause of great sorrow all round. The distance from Bembridge to Wootton Creek being over six nautical miles, and being without the benefit of engine power, Dinger and Spoofer enlisted the help of their maths teacher 'Snout'. I never knew his proper name, addressing him either as 'sir' or 'sn-ah-um'. He had a turned up nose. He had rowed at Oxford or somewhere. Mother said he had a 'refined' accent, so that was OK. He proved a pain in the butt.

He pulled one oar and I took the other. Spoofer had had mastoids and Dinger was bloody useless on an oar.

Snout said, 'If it takes one hundred strokes to propel a boat four hundred and eighty feet, assuming that each stroke takes six seconds and that there are approximately 6,070 feet to the mile, how long will it take to row six miles lads?' Between us we produced the sort of silence only found in the deepest catacomb. Snout spent the next hour with eyes closed in concentration working it out.

To greet us at the mouth of the creek, at Fishbourne, was its unofficial Harbour Mistress, Dorien-Smith. Navy-blue divided skirt, whistle, ruddy face and voice of brass. She had a *very* refined accent. During the war to come she is reputed to have straddled her own roof with a twelve bore shotgun blasting at German aircraft. She may not have posed a threat to the Luftwaffe but, by God, she worried her neighbours. She mustered half a dozen like-minded friends and hauled us out on the shingle bank.

Fitting out back in the thirties broke no banks. Tar, at threepence a bucket from the gasworks, was the basic ingredient. A man wearing a sack apron turned a spigot and out oozed this black and iridescent snake. He would hold out a hand. The pennies would stick to it. Your boots smacked stickily as you walked away.

Nowadays buying bottom-paint demands specialized knowledge, less in the matter of the product as in the matter of concealing chequebook stubs from alert wives. 'I simply *do not believe this*!' Then comes the 'scrimping and saving' bit. 'Here I am scrimping and saving for a few rags to wear and you ... YOU!' 'But Sugarplum, it works out cheaper in the long run.'

A long run would be a good idea.

Back then you lit a fire on the beach and heated it up. Any tide-line provided old tar brushes: 'long-arms', initially brick-hard but softening up with heat. You had to be wary of the weather. A rain shower and a bucket of boiling tar meant an explosion, highly dangerous, like a lot of ordinary things in those pre-nanny state times. We knew a man with a pockmarked face; we were cautious.

You added naphtha to make it dry. If you didn't you had a boat destined to leave its imprint on everything that came within its orbit. Spoof and I had once floated up-creek after tarring a skiff. Our hands were like black paws. We fended off from gleaming white enamelled yachts as we passed. Each had a paid hand aboard. Their howls and imprecations followed us into the sunset. We didn't go back for six months.

You could buy 'black varnish' which dried fairly quickly, but it cost a shilling a tin. It was for quality folk, not the likes of us. The method was to do the inside bilges first, turn her over and do the bottom, turn her back and white-paint the topsides, thwarts, gunn'les, and so forth. The waterline, due to the plank lands, ended up as a zigzag.

We were already in trouble. Cycling home with a bucket of tar on your handlebars had obvious consequences. The only thing to shift tar is butter. Spoofer and I had both raided home larders, and no forensic tests were needed to follow our trail. Mother, it seemed, was 'Not made of money, Desmond'. She scrimped and saved.

Not all clinker boats can be revived with a coat of tar. There were such unguents as tar-and-cement, tar-and-canvas-tingles, lead tingles and patches. Or, as a temporary measure until planks swelled and she 'took up', you soaped her. You kept a bit of wet soap in a sealed tin for a week until it was soft and cheesy. You knifed it into the seams to stop them leaking. As she took up, the soap squeezed out. You'd see boats leaving a wake of froth, giving a false impression of speed.

We called her '*Nighthawk*'. Lord knows why.

Nighthawk. *The walkway squirted mud straight up your trouser leg. Negotiating it was done at a mincing trot. She cost a syndicate of three of us ten bob each – but then you have to pay for quality.*

Then we rigged her. The mast was a five bob scaffold pole. Bamboo curtain poles gave us gaff and boom. A neighbour's garden had a hedge *and* three strands of wire. Soon he had two strands, and we had rigging. Woolworths, the threepenny and sixpenny store, supplied clothesline and galvanized halyard blocks. We nicked an old yacht jib which was covering a boat and chopped it around to make us a mainsail, and my Boy Scout tent opened up and, cut diagonally, made two jibs. So we had to fit a bowsprit.

I found an old coffee table in the attic which, with four large screw-eyes, a rod for pintles, gudgeons and a broomstick tiller, gave us a rudder. Two pigs of iron and two bags of shingle served as ballast and guaranteed our rapid demise should we ever capsize or swamp.

Nobody wagged a finger. Nobody sucked teeth and rattled on about safety. Lifebelts were for sea walls, piers and lifeboats, and lifejackets were for courageous lifeboatmen and were made of cork.

The launch called for rollers and all hands led by Miss Dorien-Smith and her blue serge retinue, all self-nominated experts.

'Jolly good!' she bellowed. 'One jolly good heave. All together, I say. Jolly good!'

We had the floorboards up. We watched keenly. Not a drop. Then one, two, half a dozen bright beads of water trickled, dribbled, flowed and collected to form our first very own bilge water. 'Poink, poink' went the bean tin bailers.

I had bought a book called *Learning to Sail a Dinghy*, price sixpence, possession of which made me the skipper on our first sail. It was brief and an educational feast.

We set sail, sheeted home and drifted to leeward stern-first. Then we got it together and reached up and down in style, tacking with the aid of an oar and making leeway like a top hat. The wind was offshore. Fisherman Les Warman, him of the flatty that could be rowed on a dewy lawn, towed us back. He had some technical advice for us.

'Bugger a boat that'll not go ter winn'rd!' he said. 'You needs a dagger-board in 'un.' We should have listened. But then Paul joined the syndicate with his two quid outboard and so it was all right; we could always motor back. Like pigs can fly.

An evening sail, wind offshore again which it usually was off Wootton Creek, and back and forth we sailed, pointed up hard, sailing crabwise, getting further and further to leeward and offshore. As the wave fetch increased it got rougher. There was me in charge, Paul, Spoofer and Dinger Bell. He said, 'I want to go back.' We suddenly realised that we all wanted to go back. It was time for the outboard. It was an ancient Elton Twin, horsepower unknown, not that it mattered since the bastard wouldn't start. Paul kept saying 'Strange', jerking the cord ... chuffa-chuff, 'Strange!'

Ashore the first lighted windows were twinkling. Chuffa-chuff. 'Strange!' Finally he gave up and we broad-reached, crabbed as far as Ryde Pier, crabbed back again, then again, getting further and further to leeward. It got dark; it turned bloody chilly. We got the sails down and wrapped them around ourselves, four ghosts huddled and frightened.

I felt strangely let down, betrayed by something cherished. Had I but known it I was learning a vital lesson about the sea, albeit the Solent sea – it isn't a playground but a serious and dangerous place where we sport with fingers crossed.

'We ought to signal,' Dinger said. At least we were not stupid enough to try setting light to a petrol-soaked rag. Spoofer started to pray very loudly, then we tried a hymn, *All in Peril on the Deep*. The title was the only bit we knew so we just sang it over and over again in different keys. It didn't seem very effective.

Paul had a brainwave. I had a packet of De Reske Minors. We took one each, lit them in the shelter of the sail and then all inhaled together so that there was a red glow. Four scared faces in close harmony. Dinger was sick. The Lord moves in mysterious ways.

Suddenly there came a shaft of light from the darkness. The Lord had sent us the Mew Langton beer barge *Foxhound* bound for Pompey with a cargo of best bitter. There was a great Celestial bellow. 'Give us your line and git aboard you daft young buggers!' We did so and soon discovered that there was hot cocoa in heaven, followed soon after by bacon butties.

Back home our families had received visits from police constables in trouser clips with the news that we would be on the midnight ferry from Portsmouth. The real truth never hit our non-sailing families. Mother said, 'He could have caught his death – what with his funny chest.'

5

I get a job • Meet Derek the threepenny bundle • Get another job • I have a moving experience

It cost us two quid to get the boat towed back by a beer barge, a staggering sum and, at sixteen, I was still on a shilling-a-week pocket money. Due to our hitherto nomadic life I had never had a job. I whiled away my days making model boats and roaming the seashore. I found a human skull.

I showed it to Les Warman. 'They can be made into terbaccy jars,' he told me helpfully. I showed it to my parents. I said, apologetically, 'The bottom jaw's missing.' Great consternation. It must be given a Christian burial; we must hasten to our priest. Oh, oh, oh, and so on.

Mother's phlegmatic opinion prevailed in the end and we took it back to the beach. Father, advising it to 'rest in peace', chucked it as far as he could. This didn't strike me as either restful or peaceful.

I was too old for an apprenticeship, but mother had decided upon my destiny – I was to become a wood carver and decorate cathedrals. She would show visitors my whittled figurines. 'He's got it in him,' she would proclaim. 'He's never had a lesson. He carved this with a penknife and a bent nail!' She never showed them the female dancer with the massive, over-sandpapered boobs.

She wrote around but nobody wanted my talents; perhaps church art and big boobs were incompatible. Neither was the Isle of Wight over endowed with cathedrals. I thought it a lousy idea but never considered complaining.

Meanwhile a local boatyard had room for a lad. I held the ends of planks, and carried and supported things for other men to hammer or bang. During the dinner hour, when the machinery was idle, I had to go around with an oilcan and rag, giving the grease caps a half twist.

I was on my back underneath the big band saw, oiling away, when a chap came in to do a home job. 'WHEEEEEEEEEEEEEEEEEEEEEE!'

A Funny Old Life

My squeaks went unheard. When he'd done I crawled out powdered like a shop bun. There was bloody hell to pay, and mother insisted that I withdraw my labour.

I got to know Derek, the three penny bundle, through Spoofer. He had a ramshackle boatyard of clattering corrugated iron in which he did up ancient boats and sold them to any total beginner able to stump up and who was a yachting virgin. He was a pioneer in ferro-cement – if a boat was so far gone that screws would no longer hold he built her up with concrete planks, which, when painted, would fool anybody. They say that one of Derek's creations hit Ryde Pier ... the cloud of dust caused beautiful sunsets for weeks afterwards.

'What's the threepenny bundle bit all about?' I asked Spoofer. It seemed that Derek's great pleasure in the winter was to sit chopping sticks for fire lighting, tying them up in threepenny bundles. With the bogey stove roaring, his wireless blaring, pipe in mouth and singing along in a shower of sparks and flying dottle he was happy the day long. The source of supply came from old barges which he'd break up on the mud. There had been trouble with the police. Derek had a mate in the quarrying business who had access to, but no knowledge of, blasting explosives. 'It don't need no more than a little bit,' he'd opined. The bang blew out windows over a wide area, and the rain of debris wrote off greenhouses and back door glass porches.

One Sunday morning we paid Derek a social call. We found him with his back to the kitchen fire playing a concertina. He wore an ankle-length nightshirt and his cap, and he was puffing his pipe. 'This is a hard bit,' he announced, producing an unearthly series of gross squawks and farting noises.

There was this barge up the Medina that he planned to tow back to the creek to be broken up. Would we care to come along and lend a hand? We jumped at the chance.

'One of you can man the barge and the other can handle the tow-rope. She might steer a bit heavy, but it'll be alright you'll find!' We would come to realise that 'it'll be alright you'll find' was a favourite expression and one to be regarded with the deepest possible suspicion.

The barge was in a ramshackle yard. There was an old man in regrettable trousers; you couldn't see what his legs were doing but his trousers were crouching, as if poised for a great leap. He said, 'You've come for the bar ba ba ba ...'

'Barge,' Derek obliged him.

'Well I've pu pu pu pu ...'

28

'Pumped her out, obliged I'm sure!' Ten quid changed hands and away we went.

Her tiller was a length of two-by-four. She was an old swim-head of between forty and fifty feet over all, *and I was at the helm*. Derek's 'lanch' was powered by an ex-bus engine which might have accounted for its regular stops. We made one just as we came abreast of the chain ferry which joined East and West Cowes. Like all chain ferries it was lying in wait for passing craft – such ferries wait until a vessel is committed, rumble menacingly, then leap forward to scare the hell out of a helmsman who opens up, flat out in panic.

Not us. 'That'll be alright directly you'll find!' Derek said routinely, lid up, banging about at the engine. Right in the front of the ferry – which has neither bow nor stern – with the front wheel of his bike pushing against the barrier, was the usual man in the mucky mac and flat cap.

'Piss orft out of it mate!' he advised.

The ferry driver made angry clanking noises. He raised his ramp and came at us like an iron alligator quitting its mud bank, heading for the luckless explorer in his frail dugout. The collision was inevitable. We grated and ground athwart the end of the ramp while the ferryman, dressed as for winter in the North Atlantic in sou'wester and oilies, howled vilification in concert with the man in the flat cap and the angry twitters of motorists aboard. The launch engine fired.

'That'll be alright you'll find squire!' Derek declared.

By God I felt proud, slipping downriver, helm clutched in strong brown hand, strong young eyes alert for trouble. I stood to attention past the Royal Yacht Squadron as we bore off to starboard across the tail of the Shrape for Old Castle Point.

We seemed to be going slower. Spoofer was pointing. They were both staring back. I gave them a cheery wave. Off the point we had a fair tide. We also met a bit of a chop and the hulk began plunging around and rolling. Yes, by heaven, this was what it was all about,

'Oh I must go down to the sea again ...' I croaked.

I was suddenly aware why Spoofer and Derek were staring and pointing. Derek was shouting something '... alright you'll find!' The bloody thing was *sinking*! She stuck her swim-head down, shovelled up a ton of water and sent it rushing aft along her side decks, swilling back over her after decking. I leapt high as it passed beneath me and cascaded over her transom. I waved urgently.

'Get me off,' I howled. 'The bastard's sinking!'

Derek throttled back and cupped his hands.

'She's all wood; mate, she can't sink. You'll be ...' I heard no more and neither did I need to. The engine drowned it anyway. For the next three miles I jumped. The barge was awash, barely moving, swept continually, while I jumped and cursed, jumped and howled my wrath, ignored by the cretins in the launch.

She stuck on the mud just short of the creek entrance. Derek circled back. 'We'll go and collect a bite o' lunch,' he told me. 'We'll leave you in command so's nobody steals her!'

In 1937 they were taking on hands at the shipyard in Cowes. I got taken on as a heavy labourer: not the sort of job to put on your letter heading but for a Guinea pig Third Class aspirant, it was about right. An advert might have read: no prospects, pension or company car, but the work is dirty, dangerous and totally unrewarding. The right applicant may expect to be dismembered, disembowelled, lose fingers or fall from great heights.

Curiously I loved it. I enjoyed the work which was rough and uproarious in an all-male, vulgar sort of way. My fellow labourer, Harold, had a dry humour, and our gang boss, 'Nig' Blackman, was a swashbuckling extrovert who drove us with grins and curses.

We had a long flat-bed trolley loaded with steel plates that we towed with a hook-rope, prancing and whinnying like cart-horses, Nig steering the tail end. 'Go on yer daft buggers!' And we'd go clattering and rumbling over the cobbles.

Plate hanging could be dangerous if you were not careful. A thirty-by-six foot plate would be whipped aloft by the crane. It had hook-ropes on two corners, and Harold and I would be up on the 'deals' or stagings trying to catch hold and take a turn. On a breezy day the plate could get out of control and start weaving around, figure-of-eighting. There had been a man who'd had the top of his skull sliced off, 'like a ****ing boiled egg, mate!' Somebody saved a bit of hair and bone in a matchbox.

You had to guide it down until Nig could jab a pinch-bar through two rivet holes and get a service bolt in. They were still riveting ships when I started. That was another laugh.

There was a three man team of riveter, holder-up mate and a lad on the bogey heating rivets. He'd foot-pump away and get them red hot, then sling them with his pincers to be caught in the holder-up's box. One day a swinging hook-rope picked up a bogey and whisked it skywards. There were red hot cinders and rivets flying everywhere and fellers howling. Foremen traditionally wore bowlers, the hardhat of the times. A rivet burned down right through a foreman's bowler. There he was, clutching his smoking napper, going flat out for the dock to stick his head in.

We had moved home to an old coachhouse on the empty Binstead Hall estate where we had use of a slipway and boathouse on the foreshore. During one winter we fitted deck, coamings and a dagger-board to *Nighthawk*, the latter spouting water from every joint despite soap, tar-and-cement, glue-and-sawdust and other unguents. There was a saying: 'In glue and dust I put my trust. If that don't do it then putty must.' Nevertheless she could now be tacked and worked to windward, a spectacular improvement.

An inland boating lake went bust and rowing skiffs, long neglected and with gaping seams like hungry mouths, went for thirty bob apiece. We bought three and, for two quid, a fourteen foot double-pair gig. We planned to do them up and sell at vast profit. Nobody wanted them.

We filled the boathouse with driftwood, much of it going to the construction of a wobbly jetty out over the saltings. With *Nighthawk* moored all-fours in a gully we could board her when the saltings were covered, though negotiating that swaying, lurching contraption to reach her called for spangled tights and a balancing pole.

It was the big tides that I loved. On a really big spring there seemed to come a hush. The sea lay bland, mauve, without a ripple, and there would be a hint of haze. If there was any breeze at all it seemed not to touch the surface so that under sail you glided silently with a whisper at the bow.

At the top of the tide the saltings were hidden, save for the tips of the marron grass, and you could glide hissing through it with the big green shore crabs on their hind legs, squaring up with their claw-fists: 'Right, come on then lets have yer!'

The creek became magical. The shoreline oak trees dipped skirts into the tide, becoming muddied as if they'd been supping cocoa. We could glide swift and silent in and out of gullies ordinarily dry, whisk past overhangs of tamarisk, invade private creeks, and all as if we were flying. One day we strung all our skiffs astern, a nipper in each bailing hard. 'Poink', the bailers went, 'poink poink poink', up the creek to the bridge and back again.

After a couple of years we were moving again, this time to King's

31

Quay cottage. On the Osborne House Estate it was the only cottage or habitation for miles around. It had been designed by Prince Albert, bored out of his skull and an architect by hobby. It was a ghost of Bavaria, a sugar cake cottage. It had an annexe and miniature stables, the former in recognition of an old widow's weak bladder and the latter to house the tiny ponies that drew her dog cart.

The removals man came to size up the job. None of your Pickfords for us though; this was a cut-price job, and his van looked like a covered wagon, lacking only women in poke bonnets toting Winchester rifles. He surveyed our household effects in mounting gloom.

'What you got 'ere squire,' he told father, 'is nearer your load and a narf which means charging according!'

Which was when the idea of taking stuff by boat came about. Father said, incredibly, 'The garden stuff can go by boat!' just like that. It was incredible since he'd only been in the boat once. I took him out to see the redshanks. By the time we reached them he had his teeth in his pocket, his chin on the gunn'le, and he was gazing shorewards with the longing of an Irish emigrant taking a last look at the 'auld sod'. He was a Godly man and never swore. 'Fuff the web champff!' he groaned harrowingly.

Ordinarily one associates 'garden stuff' with croquet mallets, cast iron herons and loungers. Not us. We had enough mattocks, scythes and pitchforks to arm Wat Tyler's rebellion, but the rest was organic junk: a malodorous mountain of bagged compost, bonemeal and drums of reeking mulch. There was a water butt, trays of seedlings, tomato plants in pots, raspberry canes lagged in rotting burlap, a wheelbarrow, an incinerator, sodden tarpaulins that when unrolled released a wonderland of wriggling, jackknifing insect life, and, crowning all, a rustic archway. Father eyed a mouldering sack of hoss-manure with pride. On top of all rode four bikes.

At high water we began loading *Nighthawk*, then the four skiffs. The bailers were at work already. The infant Moses in his wicker basket would have been granted an A1 at Lloyd's by comparison. There was me, Paul, Spoofer and Dinger with two more young nippers as extra bailers. Onlookers said later that we made an eerie sight. The skiffs were of low freeboard in any case ... loaded they created the bizarre picture of a wheelbarrow and a rustic arch seemingly heading seawards. It was clock-calm.

The outboard, the Elto Twin (a name implying that somewhere there must be another one exactly like it ... a disturbing thought), clattered into life, and off we went, our train straightening out astern, the last in line with a coquettish flirt of raspberry canes.

Progress was to be intermittent. That engine would run for hours in a water butt behind the shed ... clamp it on to the stern of a boat and it was like asking an infant to recite in public. When it stopped the routine was to draw your sweater arm over your fingers, remove and juggle with hot plug, wipe on seat of pants, blow on plug, pencil its points and replace it. Then came a lengthy series of permutations between choke and throttle interspersed with jerks varying in savagery and the mystic incantation of 'Right-you-bastard-this-time-then!'

Predictably the first stoppage left us athwart the Fishbourne car ferry route. The ferry went hard astern, and, on her bridge, a man in a cap gave us a wave with both fists. A breath of breeze stirred the mildewed bundle above our heads and we were under way.

We steered inshore shading our eyes, not for any navigational reason but motivated by a blend of hope and carnal desire: the wooded slopes were hemmed by high fencing on all but the seaward side and contained a secluded nudist camp. It was the target of every lascivious lout with access to a boat. I'd never seen anything but others claimed otherwise. They'd roll their eyes. 'Cor!' they'd say, using both hands, 'you shoulda seen 'em!'

A man in a deerstalker hat waved a stick at us and shouted; we sheered off. The engine was working again. Then it wasn't. We anchored. The second high water of those zany Solent tides came and went while Paul jerked and cursed; around us the skiffs lay at all angles, bailing bean tins chiming musically and continually. We, he

anyway, stripped the float chamber, blew through the jet, and emptied and strained the fuel through Dinger's hanky. The accumulated filth of a teenager's trouser pocket is the equivalent of using a Dyak's breech clout as a surgical dressing. But it worked. The throttle was wide open and the engine exploded into life. The anchor was still down. We brought up solid, the skiffs astern cannoning into each other, then we sheered hard round. There were yells, legs in the air, skiffs swamping, tomato pots afloat, pure bloody mayhem. Round and round we went until I thought of casting off our anchor line. We left a wake of cabbage leaves and prime horse muck.

We headed for Kings Quay only half a mile ahead, tried for a short cut and stuck on the mud in the now sluicing ebb tide. Stonehenge could have been shifted more easily.

We waited a couple of hours then began the long squelch shoreward. We looked like a defeated army. We should have been dragging a cannon. Father was waiting on the beach holding a bucket. It seemed a thoughtful gesture; we were plastered with mire and he'd brought some water. He spoke first. 'My tomato plants. I'd like you to nip back and give them a drop of water.' I breathed slowly, controlling my emotions. 'The tomato plants have had some water!' I said between gritted teeth.

6

A Very Special Constable • The weir-wolf • The three quid nape

The shipyard produced some prime rascals. They'd have had the pennies off a dead man's eyes; wise cadavers kept one open. Using works materials and time our yard produced ships, doll's houses, scooters, fireguards, garden gates and weathercocks – all spirited out from under the gateman's eye.

One chippy produced wheelbarrows. He then applied for a chitty to take out a sack of sawdust for his rabbits; he must have had a warren – three sacks in three brand new barrows. Then he started on doll's prams. Another syndicate of pilferers tried nicking chain by lowering it down a drainpipe into the street. It took charge; it was night and the racket brought crowds out to see if there'd been a nasty accident. Then there was the Great Vice heist.

A bench vice dismantles into two parts which can be hung round the neck under the regulation mucky mac. This matie took an order from a man in a pub: five quid, right? Right! At knock-off we escorted him to the gate. He was walking a bit heavy, sort of lurching like a mechanical man while we urged him along. 'Piss off!' he hissed. The gateman was used to funny walks and took no notice. He'd seen the erect and military gait of a man wearing a fireguard around his chest, the walking-wounded limp caused by copper piping stuffed up your trousers and the rolling waddle resulting from a tight cummerbund of forty fathoms of best manila rope.

Matie tripped and fell. He couldn't get up; he lay there cursing and hissing requests for assistance that we were too choked to render. The gateman came bustling out.

'Poor feller's had a stroke, look at 'im foamin'! Get a nambulance quick!' And he rushed back in and phoned for one himself. It arrived in minutes. We told the ambulance men the facts and about the five quid involved, nod-nod, wink-wink. It was hell's own struggle to get him and the vice on to a stretcher.

The gateman shook his head dolefully. 'Will he recover? How much will it affect him arterwards?'

'About five quid,' the ambulance man said.

When I met the Special Constable I assumed that he must be on secret service; after all, everybody knows that Special Constables are naturally law-abiding and scrupulously honest. He worked in the office, which further heightened his social standing. He'd heard that I was into boats. He just happened to have for sale this twenty-foot, ex-ship's boat, galvanized steel cabin cruiser.

My God. A cabin cruiser! A boat with a *down below*! Mankind has been looking for holes to crawl into since the dawn of time. *Homo sapiens* legging it for his cave spurred on by a pair of eight foot Mammoth tusks.

'How much?' I asked unwisely.

'Fifteen nicker. You look like a lad who knows a thing or two about boats, so I'll tell you what I'll do: make it twenty and I'll throw in the engine.'

I had an uneasy feeling that the engine is usually part of the deal when buying motorboats, but, for a boat with a down-below, well I ask you. He said the engine was up home on the bench being 'fine-tuned'. I had a mental image of a silky tick-over, growing to a throaty growl of naked power as the throttle was advanced.

'When can I take a look at the bottom?' I asked, more to show that I knew a thing or two about boats than to satisfy any technical curiosity.

He said, slowly, incredulously, a man wrestling with a novel concept in a foreign tongue, 'Take ... a look ... at the bottom?' He gave this kindly little laugh, 'but this is a *steel-built* boat son, none of your rot, none of your gribble and "toreador" worms in steel boats!' We had a good old laugh at the idea, man-to-man, trickster-to-prat.

The boat was named *Tzigane*, which he told me meant 'gypsy', a romantic notion and 'cross-me-palm-with-silver, that's a kind face yez got sur'. There was a big cockpit for fishing, rendered still bigger by the absence of the engine, then two little doors like a kitchen cabinet which gave access to 'down-below', a dank and gloomy enclosure with two shelves covered with rotting carpet. It stank like a wet Labrador. I had the floorboards up just for the look of things.

'Ah,' he said, 'sharp lad. You'll notice that her bilges are cemented out to keep her sweet and clean, just in case you ever get any water in her.' We laughed good humouredly at the idea.

Hauling Tzigane *ashore. Note portholes through which stricken observers were to see the weir-wolf and flee. OK clever dick so it's a lousy joke. 'Flee, flea', get it!*

He had her towed round to King's Quay and dumped on her anchor. He delivered the finely tuned engine by road to our little stables. First we had to haul her up to be fitted out, a case for ropes, rollers and the whole family. We got her right up on top of the strand on boxes, shored up. Then, scraper in hand, I wormed underneath, rolled my sleeve up and took a good old swipe at the weeds and assorted filth.

'None of your gribble and toreador worms in steel boats son!' The bastard had said nothing about rust. *My scraper went straight through!* I lay there dazed, appalled. I wept the tears of innocence betrayed, and then, having done so, I settled in to curse him and all Special Constables of every race and creed to hell and damnation and every form of torment, disease and final dissolution. The entire bottom was only held together by the concrete in her. It was plain that I could neither use her nor sell her to some other muffin.

Among his other eccentricities, father had a fixation about sleep. What the hell has that to do with holes in boats? the discerning reader may ask. Our cottage was buried in woods and close by the sea; the only sounds to be heard at night were the whisper of leaf, waves, and, in due season, a wealth of nightjar and nightingale. Despite his preoccupation with birds in general, these constituted a disturbance to be countered only by a stack of pillows on his earhole.

My sister bought a puppy. Then, 'God!' she thought, 'suppose it whines at night?' There was nowhere she could put it except in the stables, and they were alongside the cottage. Clever-dick brother had an idea: why not bed it down in the boat sixty yards away, shielded by the trees?

'I'll go down and lock myself in the cabin and make dog noises while you listen,' I said. It was just getting dusk.

'Right,' she said, and off I went.

In each side of the cabin there were two little round portholes. Seated within, doors closed, facing two of these holes I filled my lungs. I began with a few whimpers, then, becoming more adventurous, I tried a wolf howl. It echoed and boomed, a haunting, lonely cry hinting at snowy wastes under a gibbous moon, a sound to cause the traveller to quicken his pace fearful of the hunting pack.

'Whoooooooooo!' I howled, head back, lips pursed, 'Whoooooooooo!' Then my eyes became drawn to the portholes. At each one was framed a face, a horrified, pop-eyed male face. I cut off in mid-howl. I gave a sickly smirk and a little wave of the hand.

'Evening!' I said. 'I was just ...' But they'd gone.

Hastily I quit that cabin; I had to explain.

Two shadowy figures were legging it over the shingle for all they were worth. Now, over sixty years later, there are two blokes somewhere who are convinced that they once had an occult experience down there on that lonely beach.

The idea of girls and a boat with a cabin were closely associated, and, in the course of time, *Tzigane* became known to others as 'the confessional' due to the time I tended to spend with young females 'showing them over'. I invested in the monkey also with girls in mind, though only now do I realise and confess it. Monkey-ownership would surely set me apart from other fellows: 'Oh he's the one who owns that monkey!'

A dockie over in West Cowes owned it and wished to sell to the right buyer, which had to be me. It was called, with dismal lack of originality, 'Jacko', and the price was three quid. 'Three *quid*!' I gasped. He said, a bit tartly, 'What do want for three quid mate, King bleedin' Kong?' A powerful sales pitch. I handed the money over.

Jacko came complete with harness and a couple of fathoms of lavatory chain. He was about the size of a large whippet, brown on top, grayish underneath. 'It ain't so much your actual *monkey*, manner o' speaking,' the owner said, 'More what you might call a nape'. The nape was bloody furious and promptly scratched the bridge of my nose causing blood to rain down copiously. 'Why look,' this bastard said, 'he've really took to yer!'

Jacko rode on the crossbar of my bike, wrenching at the handlebars, all the way down to the chain ferry, me swerving all over the road, everybody turning to watch. Oh, I was going to be a smash with the girls!

During the river crossing I vacated my saddle to hold the bike and Jacko took it over. I heard people laughing. I adopted a relaxed and casual air, the man who handles animals, the trainer. When I went to mount, I found that the hairy little swine had left a huge and steaming turd on it. I began to have a suspicion that I had made a very nasty mistake.

I know now that I had bought not only a nape but an angry, sexually frustrated (Jacko was undoctored), belligerent and devious little creature. He hated children who had teased him, and he adored fly buttons ... actually, any buttons for that matter, but fly buttons were a delicacy. The scene was set.

I rigged a long ground-wire and gave him another three fathoms of bog chain so that he could range from his shelter right to the top of a pear tree. He never got his chain fouled up. He would shoot aloft then come down, looping slack chain over his shoulder. He lay in wait for buttons. Try walking by in a jacket and he'd descend like a furry bullet, grab your lapels, glare, work his eyebrows up and down, then chump, chump, chump, chump – every goddam button gone and his cheeks bulging. If you resisted he'd have you in the wrist, CHOMP!

He terrorised us all. I came home one day to find mother and sister barricaded upstairs, shouting from a bedroom window, 'Jacko's loose!'

I cornered him on the roof ridge. A long ladder, carrot in one hand, clip-hook on long line in the other: 'Good lad Jacko. SNICK.' Then it was back down, paying out scope, into the outside dunny and haul away handsome. Whim, Wham, Bang and he was in and I was out. I left him in there to simmer down, and he bloody wrecked it! Loo paper, paint, garden fertiliser, broad beans ... all the stuff you'd expect to find in a loo and all down the pan.

I took him to the Folly Inn. The landlord – old Bob Savage – was an ex-RN diver knew about monkeys. 'That's no monkey. Neither is it a nape. What you got there, my son, is an old bamboo!'

I bought Jacko a brown ale and you can't say fairer than that. He threw the empty at some chap and then settled down to masturbate – which he did with vigour and at a great rate.

Masturbating monkeys and girlfriends had no future.

I tried taking him out in a boat: dead loss. I pushed the boat out, he changed his mind, fell in between boat and beach, was *livid*, bit me in the ankle, then had my fly buttons and the bowl of my pipe (a recent affectation contributing to a manly image). The hot dottle really got him going; that nape was upset. In the end he became dangerous. Only one girlfriend met him, and she just picked him up and pulled his tail which he loved. He'd have had my throat out.

At the sight of a child - fortunately a rarity - he became screaming demented. I would have to part with him. No zoo would take him. The police said he must be put down. It was tragicomic. The man with the gun couldn't do it. Jacko took hold of the barrel with both hands and applied one eye and then the other to the bore as if carrying out an officer's inspection.

Happily, a nutter from the back of the island who had a sort of private menagerie took him on. I saw him in Newport one day. 'How's Jacko?' I asked. 'Oh fine!' he said. He hadn't any fly buttons.

7

War • *Farmhouse brawn*
• *An undistinguished soldier*

The reason why zoos were loath to take on monkeys, napes or even old bamboos was quite starkly and simply the imminence of war. It crept up on me like an assassin. I rarely saw, let alone read, a newspaper, never listened to the news on the wireless (we still didn't use the word 'radio' which had an un-english sound about it), and Pathetone News at the local cinema was pure and unadulterated propaganda read in a jokey voice. Nevertheless, our parents were erudite, educated people who held powerful personal opinions which we soaked up like a sock in a puddle.

Then one day Chamberlain said his piece about 'consequently a state of war existing etc', and made it sound about as momentous as a cancelled church outing.

Mitch, Spoofer and I bought a net-boat for a fiver – twelve foot with a tray built in aft, going cheap because she'd drowned three anglers. We bought a fifty-fathom seine net, a fleet of lobster and prawn pots, and started fishing in our spare time. Every day after work we sailed and rowed round our pots – the outboard didn't merit a petrol ration – a distance of about four miles in total. We had planned to put *Tzigane*'s engine in her but I'd laid it up. Indeed, I'd laid it up so thoroughly that the mummy of King Tutankhamen would have seemed oven-ready by comparison. I'd run it up warm on the bench, then poured lube oil into each cylinder and given it a good old whirl around; it had smelt oddly familiar. I took the tin out into the daylight and read the label; it read 'best copal varnish'.

Mitch stood six foot two, wore ancient 'good' tweeds, had a very, *very* refined accent and, as mother would have said, came from 'good stock', which implied a number chalked on his bum. And that would have been appropriate because he was a black sheep and his family just wanted him the hell out of their sight. So he fished and shot, not salmon and grouse, but lobsters and anything that moved.

41

The seine net produced a mixture but included the occasional large dogfish or angler, which was huge, floppy and hideous. I used to put them in a sack and wheel them on my crossbar to the back door of the chip shop. Once there was a fifty-pounder; I was riding, wobbling along, when the sacking parted to reveal the awesome pink genitalia to a short-sighted old lady who phoned the police. They came at the double to arrest me, 'a man with a dead body on his handlebars'.

One day we had a miserly haul of prawns. 'You take them,' I told Mitch, so he did. Lacking a bag he put them into his aristocratic tweed cap and clapped it back on his head. He caught the bus home. On it was a group of his mother's lady friends. Mitch beamed down upon them. 'Why, good evening ladies!' he cried, whipping off his cap and showering them with hopping crustacea.

Father was in good form and settled in his job at the aircraft factory. He was as nutty as ever, riding his bike with its three rear lights and its stinking, hissing carbide headlamp. He was also a prime pain to local wildfowlers: he used to wait until dusk then beat an oil drum to warn the incoming birds of the waiting guns. Nowadays they would duff him up. Back then it may have been why the rumours started about him being a spy.

Lights had been observed moving among the bushes, and, with a blackout in force, any lights shown anywhere had to be suspect. The real explanation was bloody typical. Father had read an article about bowels and how the modern position 'at stool', sitting on a loo, was all wrong; nature intended us to *squat*. First came the 'stumbling blocks', as mother named them – two large hunks of timber upon which we were supposed to place our feet, thus raising the knees. Try visiting an outside loo in the dark ... crash! The stumbling blocks were voted out. But you didn't defeat my father. He dug a trench out in the copse. Every morning, or whenever the urge came upon him which was often as his diet would have suited any herbivore, father could be seen, paper in one hand, hurricane lantern in the other, bobbing through the bushes like some sniffing Will-o'-the-Wisp heading for his trench. On wet mornings he also took an umbrella. Had Hitler known, he could have routed his bombers by father and his bobbing lantern. But what really clinched suspicions was his penchant for 'air-bathing'.

The sun may not be showing but you can still air-bathe; you can get down behind a hedge, strip off stark and air-bathe. If you also happen to be a choral singer, well, what better time is there to practise Handel's Messiah, eh? Tell me that?

One day, an old farm labourer came pedalling along on his bike, minding his own business, when suddenly he heard, 'Wonderful (one-two-three-etc)! Marvellous (two-three-etc)!'

It was probably the fact that father was beating time that upset him and convinced him that here was a German spy and therefore foreign and a bit odd. When they came the police were not so much professionally challenged as strained. They seemed glad to leave.

My call-up came. It was a relief. I had been deeply ashamed. I had promised mother that I'd wait to be called up, but I felt gutted. Unbeknown to her I had joined a civilian bomb disposal team in an effort to ease my conscience. The army were the experts; we merely dug as directed. We only got one bomb, and it turned out to be a dud.

The call-up came on a day when I had witnessed an act of faith. On a toolbox in the plate shop there was this man who healed the sick, and I'm glad I didn't miss the spectacle. The patient sat on the box, and the healer got to work on him while we looked on. The healer prodded his guts.

'That it?'

'Lower.'

'Ah!'

The healer began pummelling away like he was making bread, intoning prayers, pummelling his own guts, then back again. Then he struck pay-dirt.

'AHHHH!' howled the patient. 'Right, that's enough mate, I'm cured!'

And, so saying, he leapt up whamming his head into a shelf then sinking inert with a hollow moan. You don't see faith like that every day.

My army career was to prove anticlimactic but fairly typical in terms of farce and cock-up. I quickly rose to the rank of Lance Corporal which, in terms of promotion, is like standing on a thin book. We were on a training exercise on the Yorkshire moors. I had command of a squad of blokes whom I didn't know, and, with all the innocence of Little Bo Peep, I failed to list their names.

'Take cover and spread out lads!' I ordered commandingly. Every son of a bitch vanished into the bracken never to be seen again ... by me at any rate. I was alone; nearby there was a farm. 'Drink of water,' I thought, heading for it.

There was this scarlet-faced woman in sacking and a man's trilby. She said, 'I've got summat for thee lad', and led me indoors. Great! I thought, spot of the old bacon and eggs for certain! She left me sitting squared up to the table. She was back in a minute and smacked a plate down in front of me. 'There you are then. Real home-made farmhouse brawn. Don't be frightened to eat it all.' And with that she left me to it.

Frightened? I was petrified. That brawn sat there and *shuddered*. It was a mass of little tubes and nodules like some hellish scientific experiment, a microscope slide revealing God-alone-knew what mutations of disease. I looked around for somewhere to hide it. There was a stuffed heron in the fireplace. The window? Yes, the window. It was stuck, painted in solid.

She was back. 'How's it going down, lad?'

'Mmmmm!' I said, forearm over it, rolling my eyes with ecstasy. She left. I tried the heron, managed to stuff a bit of that nauseating compound up its tail but not enough. God! She was coming back! I shovelled it into my handkerchief and stuffed it down the front of my battle-dress blouse. As long as I bowed my shoulders forwards to relieve the pressure on it I was OK. She came in.

'Lovely!' I lied, smiling a ghastly smirk. 'Can't begin to thank you (true) but must fly, ha, ha. Troops waiting. Bye!' And I scuttled out, loping along in an ape-like gait, arms swinging forward. Only to meet the Platoon Commander.

'Stand up man!' he roared. '*Get those shoulders back!*'

I did so, slowly, feeling that foul comestible spreading, moulding itself like some unthinkable poultice over my chest and around my ribs.

It was an undistinguished military career, inglorious with the war half over – the raspberry that runs out of breath. I should have stayed with my hook-rope. I should have stuck to my uniform of steel-capped boots and mucky mac instead of going into itchy khaki. But let's examine some military vignettes.

It was a PT session, knickers, vests and ammo boots. We stood in a line waiting to shin up a rope. I yawned widely and my jaw jammed open. There I stood, eyes rolling, saliva drooling, making gutteral grunts. The PT sergeant, an old Indian Army man, saw me.

'Dear God, 'tis the rabies!' he howled. 'Two of yiz get him down to the MO at the double, GO!'

I heard this diagnosis and took off like a hound from the slips, my attendants following a poor second. Straight across the sacred parade ground, past the officers' mess where I swung up a wild salute to an astonished and bibulous old major, straight into the sick bay and the presence of the MO, bypassing a queue of squaddies with their pants around their ankles.

'What the bloody hell ...!' cried the MO technically, rising to his feet.

My jaw, quietly, without fuss, closed. I said, 'Please sir, I've got rabies!'

I had one pip; long-service squaddies addressed me as 'sir' after a millisecond pause. I had commandeered a launch on a small and unimportant river. My sort-of batman, Private Lore, was prone on the sun-shelter behind the Bren in his knickers, singing 'Some enchanted evening'. In the water, also in my knickers but plus beret and gun-belt, I was fixing the rudder ... 'I will come and find you!' I finished, rising from the water with a flourish.

'What the HELL is going on here!' roared the Brigadier.

Once, a myopic marksman fired at me. He hit a tree.

The train was clicking along when a mine exploded. It left the track in a screeching of steel, steam and screams. It came to rest. We scrambled through windows brandishing guns. I thought, 'This is it! This is the shooting war!' There was nothing to see. Just a dying soldier, *half* a dying soldier.'

I should have held his hand. It has haunted me for all the years that have passed, and it will always haunt me.

Tragicomedy. There was the jump. 'Stand in the door. GO.' I landed in a gorse bush and was stuck full of more prickles than a sea urchin. 'Look what you've done to your 'chute man!' the instructor bitched.

I left the war unscathed, with not a scratch save for a small scar on my left wrist which I won tripping over a latrine bucket in the dark. It was a full latrine bucket. It was fitting.

At the de-mob depot they gave me a brown suit, brown shoes and a brown trilby which blew off. 'Sod it!' I said, and I gave it to Oxfam.

Gainful employment • Tore-outs • Big hats prove nothing • Literary urges

The rebirth of yachting was more of a reincarnation. Throughout the war years the yachts of peace lay in draughty sheds, drying out, opening up, or they were left out under flogging tarpaulins, sheerlines sagging. Others lay in mud-berths, some to survive (albeit bleached as old bones), others to fall over, fill, become a tenement for crabs. You'd see their masts: angled and with a banner of frayed rope cracking in the wind. Often their gear was in store; spars conker-bright, teapot and telescope, all going for peanuts to pay off the storage bill.

You could buy a huge old hull – her lead ballast keel sold for scrap so that she floated high as a bottle, swaying – for next to nothing just to clear the debt of an owner who would never return. Syndicates of young men, dreaming of South Sea Islands and girls in grass skirts, prowled the saltings looking for their dream boat. There was one lot who bought a hulk, moved aboard and, as top priority, settled down to master the Hawaiian guitar.

Then there was the DSCD (Director of Small Craft Disposals). The boats lay rafted up by the hundred at points around the country. Fairmiles, motor-gun or torpedo boats, requisitioned yachts, barges and trawlers. Everything from ships' lifeboats to tugs. You went and looked, made an offer, and waited.

Derek allegedly looked over a Fairmile B, secretly drilled a few small holes in her and then put in an absurdly low bid. The DSCD fell about laughing. A week later they looked out of the window; she was six inches by the head! Derek's bid was accepted. Boot-faced he paid up and took possession. He had a pocket full of little wooden plugs known in the trade as 'snottle-dogs'.

Meanwhile I was taking great pains to keep from signing on at the Labour Exchange. Unless classified as 'gainfully employed' you might end up as a Bevin boy down a coalmine. We fished a bit, raked a few

46

cockles, and we did the odd yacht delivery – we being me, Spoofer and Jim Salmon, newly demobbed from air sea rescue.

The snag was that we got the tore-outs. There were scores of bright young ex-naval officers with clean-cut features dashing around with the class stuff while we, with our shaky qualifications, collected the creaky-leakies. We also came cheap.

There was a little Solent Sunbeam, a small racing keel-boat class, which Spoofer and I sailed from Solent to Falmouth. 'Return fares paid, tenner each, a doddle!' Spoofer said. We had a Lilo and a sleeping bag under the foredeck, which we were to share watch-and-watch. Away we went, wind off the land, going like the clappers. This is the life.

I had first watch below. I also had a sheath knife on my belt with its point protruding. 'Me for a spot of zizz then', I cried, crashing down with a sigh of contentment and a hiss from the Lilo.

By midnight we had Portland Bill on our starboard quarter. The wind veered and came astern. It came on to blow a bit. When we tried to take a couple of tucks down the halyard jammed. There followed a wild, scary sleigh ride – bow-wave like an elephant's ears, non-stop panic, until we got under the lee and hauled Spoofer up to fix it.

We arrived at Falmouth totally whacked. The owner said, 'Never expected you to get here so soon!' I hadn't expected to get there at all.

When Spoofer's mum stumped up the cash to buy the sixty foot motor barge, she said she was 'investing in his future'. She should have stuck to the Woolwich. Idiots had fitted an ex-WD high-speed engine converted to paraffin which produced three knots, a rooster-tail of cavitation, and a racket that set every dog within five miles howling.

'We'll get free gravel from the Portsmouth channel dredgers; builders are begging for it,' Spoof enthused, painting a picture of grateful builders sobbing their gratitude. How could it go wrong?

She was moored off the Folly Inn on the Medina where we (with uncanny foresight) downed a couple of pints apiece prior to getting under way. Spoofer nursed his engine while I steered. In our wake we left this shattering din, a pall of smoke, and people shading their eyes. Predictably, fists were shaken as we passed down river. I bore away for Castle Point and rounded it with a glow of pride. And a warm bum.

Behind me the whole bloody bulkhead was on fire. The exhaust pipe was routed up the rear of the wheelhouse and it was uninsulated;

consequently the paintwork had blistered, bubbled and popped like some foul omelette, and finally burst into flame. I belted aft.

'Fire, fire, FIRE!' I cried unoriginally.

Spoofer popped his head up, deafened but grinning happily. He gave me a thumbs-up.

'We're on FIRE, you stupid bastard!'

His gaze wandered past me to the now-billowing smoke. He vanished and the engine was cut dead. Now the problem was simple: we had no extinguisher. Spithead was full of water and we had a bucket, but its lanyard was too short. It was the sort of problem that confronts Young Executives on a management course ... 'Oh let me sir!' The solution was simpler still. Four pints of best bitter simple. We stood shoulder-to-shoulder, elbow-to-elbow and hosed out the fire using a technique mastered in foul competition as schoolboys.

Having stopped the engine nothing short of necromancy would restart it, so we accepted a pluck from a passing fellow barge skipper to the mouth of Wootton Creek where we anchored on a tatty bit of rope. Spoofer rowed ashore for his tools.

It was dusk by the time the engine resumed its hellish din; we got our anchor and headed up-creek. There was a local fishing boat moored in the channel. I was shaping a course to pass it, we had a fine, fat flood under us ... but something odd was happening up forr'd. The rope lay where we had dropped it in our haste. It was *moving*; I watched as it snaked across the deck, up over the bulwarks and vanished from sight. An awful thought struck me! 'No, NO!' I gasped, dashing forward too late.

The rope led down and aft. It was thrumming like a harp string. There came a deep, resounding CLUNK and the engine stopped for the second time that dreadful day. Spoofer arrived just in time for the final act.

We drifted down alongside the fishing boat. The barge *leaned upon* it like some drunk in a pub. The boat up-ended itself, and then, with a hollow rumble and thud, it disappeared under our bilge and under our bottom,

48

re-emerging briefly with a jaunty nod prior to vanishing completely. 'Maybe nobody saw!' Spoofer said pleadingly. Believing in fairies.

Jim and I took on a mid-January delivery of a lifeboat conversion from Burnham-on-Crouch to Chichester Harbour. Fifty quid flat, split it down the middle. We took an ex-RAF grid compass, charts and sleeping bags, and the rest on trust; it was akin to shooting Niagra in a barrel. It was witheringly cold, and snow was beginning to fall. Our cupidity matched our stupidity.

She was ketch-rigged and the yard man said she'd been 'fitted out for the passage', which suggested a team of craftsmen busy with spike and spanner but meant that he'd bailed the dinghy. We suffered a night of frigid misery, then Jim got the engine going after a lot of cranking and cursing. We were away as dawn was breaking. The sky looked like a split sack leaking mud.

It took us all day to navigate across the Thames Estuary, via the guts and swatchways, in a dismal murk peppered with snowflakes. To keep warm we sat below with the paraffin cooker going and the grid compass on the table aligned with a crack. We steered with tiller-lines, a line each.

We made North Foreland in the early dusk. I'd elected to go outside the Goodwins, not caring much for the muddled prickle of lights in the Gull Channel. It was a long, long horrible night. The wind freshened southerly. The mizzen blew out and then the jib, both ripe as cathedral banners. She wouldn't tack without a touch of engine to boot her through stays. Every hour or so we had to haul the dinghy alongside and bail it out.

We were doing an hour about. I was on and I shuddered continually; had I not been young and fit I would have ended up in my box. I was lethargic with misery. I just steered numbly, guiltily aware that I hadn't looked at the chart in ages, hadn't checked the tidal stream, just headed 'westish' and, like St Paul, 'longed for daylight', as if that would make a spit of difference.

There were the usual sailing sounds: the boom and surge, the wind wuthering through our sparse rig, chop of bow-wave, the creak of rudder. Then came another sound in my head, deep down. A low, remote rumble, like the approach of an underground train.

While I pondered I saw something ahead. It looked like a wall, pale, low down. A quayside? Then I realised that it was moving, rising and falling ...

'Jim, JIM. Come up quick!'
The line of surf drew closer by the second.
Jim took a look. 'Christ!' he said in prayer, not blasphemy. He rammed in the starting handle. He cranked and swore. The engine was dead.

The line of breaking surf looked desperately close, too close for me to attempt a tack. To miss stays would be fatal. We were too close to risk paying off and gybing her round. Jim had the spanners out. I fought down the urge to tell him to hurry. My nerves screamed ... Jim was one of those unflappable people. He had a torch tucked under his chin. Hurry, hurry, for God's sake. Hurry!

Then the engine fired; it roared, it screamed, it belched smoke and I slammed home the gear, leaning on the helm, forcing her round, seeing the bows leap and plunge! For twenty minutes I drove her flat out, bucking and rolling, back over our reciprocal. Then Jim pointed behind me and shouted something. I looked round. There was smoke pouring out of the stern locker. It was a two-tier locker, petrol tank in the upper space, exhaust exit in the lower. I knew instantly what was happening. My scalp went tight. There was rope and stuff in that lower locker – and a red-hot exhaust pipe! History was repeating itself like bad joke.

Jim had found the fire extinguisher; banged the knob ... *nothing happened*. Meanwhile, stupidly, I'd flung open the locker door. Smoke was replaced by a gush of flame ... Jim cut the engine, 'Bucket!'

We tore open lockers. Where the hell was it? How about the loo bucket?

No bloody lanyard on it ... Tail of jib sheet. Moral: don't just *learn* knots but learn to make them flat out, at night, in panic!

Soon afterwards, the fire extinguished, cooling pump fixed again, we saw a big freighter passing. We noted her heading and followed her. We fetched Dover by mid-morning, berthed, fed grossly ashore, then slept.

So far this narrative has been steely-grey stuff; it was time for a cock-up.

We were towing a dinghy (no inflatable tenders in those days) off Dungeness with a following wind and sea. We started learning the technique. A dinghy lags back while the yacht surges ahead on a wave crest. Bang! The dinghy brings up solid with spray buzzing from the painter. The yacht stops and the dinghy roars up on a crest and boots you up the butt. This sequence is repeated endlessly like country dancing; you need bells on your knees and tassels. But there *is* an end. We tried varying the tow length to get her riding the third wake wave like it says in the books. She sheered off and stopped, half-filled. We rounded up and, at great risk, rove a second painter through the ringbolt in her stem.

'Right,' says I. 'Get away from *that* you bastard!' which was a pity. It was evening when we motored up to Birdham. The owner spotted us and all was sweetness, handshakes all round.

'Well done lads!' he beamed. Then his smile began to fade. He said, deadly quiet, 'Dinghy?'

'Ah, well, yes and no, in a manner of speaking.'

Jim, on cue, held up the ends of the twin painters. They were attached to a ringbolt, and a large splinter.

In 1948 I met 'Chunky' Duff, the man who was to teach me my seamanship and to provide a life long role model. He was a yacht surveyor, an ex-gunboat skipper, stocky, swarthy, and possessing that special Western Isles charm and mysticism. Spoofer had met him in Chichester at Birdham Pool where Chunky Duff had his base. He had a small charter motor cruiser on his books and needed a skipper. Spoofer didn't fancy it, and, with unusual generosity, he tendered my name.

The motor cruiser lay in Portsmouth. She was maybe forty feet long, cabins fore and aft, wheelhouse/saloon amidships. She had twin Handy-Billy engines with an exhaust note like popping porridge.

I laid her alongside at the Portsmouth ferry pontoon. The charterer was wheelchair bound; he had a private nurse built like a Grenadier Guardsman in drag and there was a nanny in charge of two kids. Their mother was a boney woman who addressed me as 'Icy Skippah'.

'Icy Skippah,' she'd say, 'when will we get to Cowes?' There was also Raymond.

Raymond was weedy and indoor-looking. You could have slit open letters with his nose. He had this Magic Hat, a yachting cap produced from a bag as if performing a trick. It fitted like a saucer on a jam jar, and it had one of those detachable white pique tops for summer, reminiscent of those worn by small boys with ringworm. The moment he put it on he became transformed.

'Right then Skippah, stand by to cast off!' he barked. I took the wheel and looked at him balefully.

Portsmouth being a naval port, the signal station at the harbour entrance was constantly a'flicker with signal lamps. Flags shot up and down. Raymond, at my elbow by the wheel, became very excited,

'Slow down, slow down man. Can't you read morse?'

'No', I said.

'God!' he said. He rushed aft, dipped our tiny ensign, then saluted. The signals were intended for the destroyer coming up astern of us. It blew a raspberry.

The nanny was dishy. She wore a floaty summer frock. She took her charges up on the foredeck. I gulped, pop-eyed. Madam was on to me, 'Jennifer, come back at once. Skippah can't see!'

Oh yes he could.

Raymond was no seaman; he coiled ropes between finger and thumb as though folding napkins. I handed over the helm outside the harbour. It was a mistake; he had me dashing around taking bearings of every buoy and landmark plus a sounding off the Gilkicker. We proceeded smack up the middle of the big-ship channel with a liner bellowing astern.

Cowes for lunch. I tried to get the wheel off him ... no way.

'Take some soundings, skippah, quick, quick man!'

Bang up the middle, me heaving a leadline. We drew about two feet six and a wet sock. The mortification of it – I had mates in Cowes. I pulled my woolly cap down and my sweater neck up.

'Mark wuff, wuff wuffle,' I cried usefully. We anchored, despite my advice, athwart the ferry route.

'*We* will be eating *our* lunch in the deck saloon,' her boniness told me, implying that, presumably, I would be having mine out of sight and from a nosebag.

It was a terrible week. Raymond covered the chart with little wig-wams and steered mid-channel. By the end of it I was a nervous wreck. Nowadays I would have applied for counselling.

When they left, tightwad father tipped me the equivalent of a handful of Dolly Mixtures. They also left me half a tin of sardines.

'You and I are going out for a little drink this evening', the Grenadier Guardsman told me, reading my expression as I examined the contents of my palm.

The boat was moored off Gosport. I rowed across to the Pompey side and left the dinghy at the pontoon – which you could do in those days without getting the oars nicked. It was an unforgettable evening.

'I don't wanna set the world on fi-yer ...' I bawled, arm draped around her shoulders, legs like rhubarb. She poured me into the dinghy. She could have drowned me, the silly old bat, but I got back to the boat, got aboard, made fast the painter with no fewer than six hitches and fell asleep on the companion-way steps.

The next charter was to a Commander RN Ret in Chichester Harbour. He just wanted to potter up and down the creeks with his wife and two kids. He came aboard and at once *put on this huge cap*! Obviously he was the Real Thing. I relinquished the wheel at once, avoiding any references to which side buoys should be left and that sort of elementary stuff.

We chuffed up to Bosham and back to Thorney Channel for lunch, the plan being to anchor for the night off East Head later on. The tide was flooding, and he took us into the channel. There are drying banks both sides of it, and to starboard there is an extensive barrier of rotting stumps plainly visible at half-flood, which it was at the time. We anchored for lunch.

It was all very easy and pleasant. After lunch we got under way, me getting the anchor and then washing down the deck. The tide was high by then, and the saltings were covered by a glassy expanse, spiked by the tips of marron grass. It was a pleasant, calm, sunny day; the Commander at the helm sang happily. I went below. Madam was washing up.

'Leave that, go on deck and enjoy the trip,' I said jovially and prattishly, happy to delegate. The engines poppity-popped, and the dinghy towing astern went slap, slap, slap.

CRASH!

Bows up, stern down, rumble, rumble, crunch; bows down, stern up, and we stopped dead.

The stumps being covered he'd gone right over the top. We were way outside the marked channel. Then it was 'pantomime time folks', and here come those laughable clowns.

'I think we hit something!' he said – a man of keen discernment, not easily fooled.

I had the floorboards up. Water was welling up like a wishing well. There was plenty to wish for. All that was missing were gnomes with fishing rods. Plainly the damage was terminal: we were sinking.

'Beach her!' I howled, pointing to a bit of shingle across the river and half a mile ahead.

He opened her up flat out. I rushed below and began pumping.

Lady-wife was using her initiative. She had the kids in life jackets, and she was cramming stuff into a large suitcase. I wasn't gaining on the water. The fly-wheel was throwing up a fan of spray. I had a good view of the debacle.

She lugged the suitcase aft to the little stern deck. It was gagging on an assortment of garments as if from a surfeit of riches. She put it down to use both hands on the dinghy painter. It was like watching a bad whodunnit; it was the butler.

'No!' I screamed. She couldn't hear me.

With the dinghy hard up to our transom she let go, grabbed and hurled the case just as the dinghy fell astern. The dinghy trundled straight over the top. The suitcase opened like some exotic bud bursting into flower. We beached leaving a wake of pyjamas, socks and bras!

I was the skipper, so I was to blame. Chunky heard me out. 'What with him being a Commander and ...' I faltered. He said sleepily, 'My dear old Des, he was a "Paybob", a desk sailor!'

I went home for a weekend to mourn and eat crow, and, while still engaged, to sow the seeds of my own destiny.

When I was a lad, model aeroplanes were made of sticks and oiled silk, and they had huge propellers powered by rubber bands that took an unconscionable time to wind up. You launched them skywards, they buzzed briefly, stalled and nose-dived into grandad's freshly planted seedbed. It all paralleled my first brief and doomed literary flight.

My sister had a stack of women's magazines. They contained ads for what the Trade called 'foundation garments'. There were suspender belts with more topping lifts, swifters, downhauls and reef points than *Cutty Sark* – all gripping stuff for the randy reader – but my attention was caught by the 'Nurse Nora' features, dedicated to readers' gender problems. There were husband-and-secretary larks and adolescents with spots. 'How-far-should-I let-him-go?' asked a maiden from Slough. The more I read the more convinced I became that I could write juicier problems than those. There was a payment of a guinea for each letter published.

'Dear Nurse Nora', I wrote happily. 'Since my husband returned from the Far East his sexual demands have been *peculiar* ...'

I became a teenager with a suspected bun in the oven, my boobs were too big, my boobs were too small, I was frigid, I was a howling nympho.

I wrote to three different magazines, permutating my problems. The guineas came rattling back and my brief writing career had begun. The editors rumbled me in the end and blasted me off the face of the earth, but it was a start.

Chunky Duff introduced me to his seventy foot gaff schooner *Hoshi*. She took my breath away. I swept my eye along her sheer, along her bowsprit, which soared aloft along luff of jib and slant of gaffs in one glorious freehand curve. We went sailing. Hard on the wind her bows peeled back the sea like scissors through silk.

Chunky said, 'We'll see how it goes. Later on there may be a job as mate if you'd like it.'

9

*The lodger game • Sleepwalkers • A horse
and cart to starboard • 'Fire, fire' • I use my
initiative*

It was 1947 and the next two seasons were learning time. I
shipped as mate aboard *Hoshi* and we went a-chartering.

Outright charters are bondage. If you get an amenable charterer
who knows nothing and is willing to be trundled around by a
skipper who calls the shots, that's fine. Others may treat you as
furniture. You'll get wealthy buffoons who just want to show off
'their' yacht to all their friends. A skipper has no option but to take
them out to where the sea is roughest and bang them around a bit.

Individual lodgers are best; divide-and-rule. You can manipulate a
crew of singles. Take fresh water: people accustomed to turning on
taps and flushing the loo give no thought to a tank which has to be
topped up, so you half-plug the breather pipe and slow the tap to a
trickle. A charterer would *demand* water.

The value-for-money punters who want to cram in the maximum
number of ports for the minimum number of days would get the
barometer scam. There is a little screw which adjusts the reading
plus or minus. 'My God!' you cry, 'Have you seen the glass? They
look. It is reading the sort of low that might precede Armageddon,
so they are happy to stay in port, eat cream teas and admire the
Municipal floral clock.

We ranged the Brittany coast and islands where engineless sailing
tunny-boats were still in use – huge beamy vessels with hunks of
railway line seized to their gaffs and chain luffs on headsails to
ensure that sails came down at the run when they shot a harbour
mouth. If you were in their berth you weren't there long. You ended
up flat and long. Chunky, regardless of expense, equipped us with
old motor tyres as fenders; he approved highly of working craft.

We had a client who walked in his sleep. We didn't guess to begin
with. At sea, on night passage, he'd come up on deck and amble

56

around mumbling. When we finally rumbled him I rigged a 'wake-up' line athwart the forehatch from whence he emerged. It caught me and nearly tore my goddam ear off. At the end of the cruise his wife left a fat tip. 'He's been run down,' she confided. 'It's made a new man of him', (hinting at a road accident of spectacular severity). 'Why,' she continued in a whisper, '*he was beginning to walk in his sleep would you believe!*'

There was a very diminutive Indian lady doctor who took to lounging on a pile of cushions on the chart table in our open-ended dog-house. Chunky didn't have the heart to tell her she had her delectable butt on sheet 2450 Beachy to St Albans. We went to Hamble instead.

Coming out of Trouville, with the lock gates shut behind us, our engine packed in. So we tried to cast off to port and sail her over the shallows, which we hit with a thump that brought everybody to their knees.

On a flat shore you should let go the anchor at once – waves come in all sizes and the bigger ones lift and dump you further on. We didn't do this. At low water a man drove round us in a horse and cart. This would have been the nadir of ignominy had it not been capped by the mother who dropped her infant's pants in the lee of our rudder.

We were neaped for a week; our party went home by ferry leaving us to bump and bang or lie on our ear. Eventually a salvage tug dragged us off across the sand into deep water. It also drove our rudder up into the trunk so that the wheel stuck up like a daisy. We were towed to Le Havre where a yard fixed it, which took another week.

We were broke. We collected wine bottles that were redeemable, and they kept us in bread and garlic sausage. Garlic is a protection against witches, which doesn't surprise me; back, back, foul harpies. We sailed the schooner home to Chichester watch-and-watch.

The following winter Spoof and I helped crew a big ninety ton ketch-yacht from the Clyde to Falmouth. She'd been bought by a syndicate who were planning to take her down to the Mediterranean to join in the cigarette smuggling racket from Tangiers. It was the current method of making a fortune, and we'd hoped to go with them. Luckily the plan fell through. The Mafia had taken over with fast gunboats and automatic weapons. Rival craft ended up like watercarts.

It was an eventful passage in any case. We fitted her out next to a DSCD flotilla of ex-naval craft awaiting disposal. There was a night-watchman in a little hut on guard against pilferers. Every night, every hour, on the hour he would open his door, stand there taking the air, collect his bottled bribe, wait for five minutes, then retreat back inside. It was regular as a cuckoo clock.

There was a gap in the chain-link fence, and a constant stream of malefactors scuttled in and out on hands and knees. The nocturnal racket of hacksaw and pipe-wrench sounded like Santa's Workshop. We got a pair of navigation lights, a ventilator cowl and a sea-anchor – the latter was destined to be my undoing at a later time.

It was January when we sailed, and it blew like hell in the Irish Sea. We hammered south and finally hove-to on starboard tack off the north Cornish coast. It was black and bitterly cold with driving rain. Then the murk cleared, a shard of moon appeared, and we found we were close inshore under the cliffs. It was patently obvious that we should go about and stand off on port tack.

We were due for a spot of drama. We discovered that the lee shroud bottlescrews had walked back and were on their last threads, wobbling to and fro like knitting needles. We daren't tack until they'd been swigged up hard or we would lose the mast.

We worked in the light of a gibbous moon with rags of cloud hurtling across it. We even dropped our only spanner! All we lacked was Dracula or rabies. With the ketch rolling hard down, men groping about on deck, wan torchlight and the cliffs to leeward, mother would probably have worried about my chest.

Having got out of that lot and rounded Land's End the weather eased and the wind fell to a flat calm. Conditions were ideal for Fire at Sea. The engine set fire to some oily rags off the Manacle Rocks (where else?). 'Fire, Fire!' cried our engineer, a stickler for convention, bobbing up from the smoke that was billowing out of the engine room hatch.

The old man, blocking the way for those who were fleeter of foot, shuffled below for the fire extinguisher and wrenched it, complete with the bracket to which it was rusted and the board to which the bracket was screwed, straight off the bulkhead. Back he lumbered, brandishing it high and, with a cry of 'Take this', whacked it down just as the engineer stuck his head up for air. He vanished with a groan.

The engine, being petrol/paraffin and having stopped on paraffin, wouldn't start again. It was a flat calm. 'Dong!' went the Manacles buoy. There we were, fanning the engineer's brow and patching his skull, drifting towards the Manacles, with the old man stomping up and down blaming fire extinguishers, which they 'don't make like they used to'.

A fishing boat towed us into Falmouth for the fee of a drum of fuel. Her skipper said, 'Cor bugger we'm losn' fesh'n toime!' and opened up flat out. They cast us off while heading for the dockside. We were carrying way like a destroyer. It was time to use my initiative, which is about as fraught with potential disaster as time-expired gelignite but a different colour. There was the fated sea-anchor, a large conical canvas bag designed to act as a drag and hold a vessel head-to-wind in an emergency. We had emergencies the way hedgehogs have fleas. It was all ready with a coil of rope bent on. I heaved it overboard. The rope began snaking out just as the old man stepped back into the coil. Spoof and I were on the next train home.

Note The yacht was later bought by the outward bound sea school where I was destined to meet her again.

Good girls don't go down sail lockers • Remoter control • Force ten and in command • Crash went the loo

We did one-week local cruises, and it was on one of these that I met Joyce Blanchard and Biddy Smart of the fledgling magazine *Yachts and Yachting*.

We sailed in relaxed fashion around the Solent, into Newtown Creek, back to Hamble, up the Beaulieu river. At anchor one evening everybody else remained below because it was a bit chilly, but Joyce and I stayed on deck. *'Pray father give me absolution for I am indulging in mucky thoughts.'*

'We could go down the sail locker,' I suggested, a bit falsetto. I lifted the circular lid. She peered down. It was like some dreaded oubliette.

'I think *not!*' she said firmly, nobody's fool, little realising that within a very few years the sail locker was to become her marital heritage.

I was still doing the occasional delivery job. There was a motor cruiser to take round to the upper Thames; she was an inland-waters boat with a hull shape like a horizontal grandfather's clock.

My crew was a motor mechanic known to all as 'Mister A'. He had a small, spherical head and a wide, permanent and apparently painted-on smile; it was the sort of head at which people shy wooden balls in fun fairs and which bobs up again, still smirking.

When 'in company' he was very correct. 'I 'aven't hany knowledge of yachtin',' he said, beaming as though at a side-splitting joke. 'I'm a hengineer pure and simple.' His purity and simplicity were never put to the test, but, by God, he was thick.

The boat was very low-power, being intended for river and canal where a great curling wake is abhorred by all and by water rats in particular. My plan was to 'catch the train': the tides divide in Dover Straits so that you can carry a flood up-Channel and then pick up the north-going ebb into the Thames Estuary. It just means getting your speed right.

Mister A proved well able to steer a course, so I got my head down during the afternoon, woke around six, cooked us a meal and then took over for the night passage around the North Foreland and 'over the land' as the inshore passage along the Kent coast was known by bargemen.

The plan was to pick up the new owner from Westminster pontoon next day at 11am, so we had time to kill. Joyce lived in Leigh-on-Sea; we could bring up there and I could nip ashore to see her.

We anchored in the Ray, a lagoon of deep water off Leigh. I didn't want Mister A cramping my style.

'I thought I might just slip ashore for half an hour and visit my young lady,' I said casually. The 'young lady' bit was deliberate. That was what he'd have called her, 'my young lady'.

'Oh,' he said, 'very nice I'm sure. I'll come with you. I wouldn't mind stretching the old legs.' I thought, 'Yes, and I wouldn't mind stretching your old neck!'

I rowed us ashore and called at the pub for directions.

'I won't be long,' I told Mister A with great deliberation. 'You'll be alright here won't you?'

'I'm not what you'd call a great drinker,' he said, raising the hand of denial. 'Except maybe a little port at Christmas, so I'd rather look round.' He could have looked any damn shape he chose.

It was really cosy. Joyce sitting one side, me the other, and Mister A between us, cloth cap on knee, saucer in one hand, cup in the other with finger correctly crooked. He ate a chocolate digestive and drank at the same time, no mean feat while smiling.

'Well, this is nice!' I said in an aching silence. Joyce agreed that 'Yes, it was nice wasn't it', which was about as passionate as it got. Mister A smirked.

We went up-river on the flood at a smacking pace and reached Tower Bridge. Things were going eerily well ...

with every bowl of custard you get a free electric fan. The steering cable snapped just as we approached the bridge. Suddenly the wheel lost bite, and we began curving off to starboard.

'The steering's gone!' I cried, banging the throttle shut.

Mister A might have been a social oik, but he was red-hot in a mechanical emergency. He had locker tops off and his biggest Mole grip clamped on the rudder post in seconds flat. With me yelling instructions we got her alongside a moored lighter.

Before starting we had checked over the steering gear; the cables were rusty. I had committed a cardinal error – there is no such thing as *good enough for the passage*. We had neither spare cable nor bull-dogs for repairs. 'If we can get her to Westminster landing stage we can get help,' I suggested.

'How long will that take though?' asked Mister A worriedly.

'Damned if I know. Hours I expect.'

Mister A's merry grin was hanging by a corner.

'The Lady-Wife and me are supposed to be 'aving The Mother-in-Law for supper.' It sounded rich fare involving bagpipes and an orange in her mouth.

Our lash-up worked quite well. Mister A crouched aft holding the Mole grip, watching my signals. I had a small flag staff behind my back which I wagged port/starboard like a dog's tail. We started nice and easy with an eye to dropping alongside another raft of moored lighters if things went awry. Once he got the knack of not over-steering we got along fine and in due course went alongside the stage and tied up to wait. I had an idea.

'Need we say anything to the owner? What do you reckon?'

He pursed up, sucked teeth, then nodded, thinking of the Lady-Wife's mother! He shuddered visibly.

The new owner arrived in bowler, pinstripe and umbrella, all beams and handshakes. 'Fine, fine, fine!' he said. 'Let's get going. Lots of hurry, must get going!' and with that we were off.

He stood, legs astride, turning his useless wheel this way and that while behind him, anticipating his movements I wagged my tail. Back aft Mister A repeated my movements.

'Steering feels a bit sloppy,' the owner said, sawing away.

'A remote control system,' I explained, wagging desperately, praying the Mole grip would stay on.

Surprisingly we actually got there. Less surprisingly the owner was bloody furious when I broke it to him.

I had my first and only experience of Storm Force 10 heading home across Channel with twenty miles to go for the Nab Tower off the approaches to Spithead. It was late evening, the forecast had been gloomy but not too alarming, but it was heavily overcast with a spit of rain. The wind was moderate on our port quarter. Another three hours or so and we'd be over Chichester bar.

Then the barometer went down in a succession of jerks.

Chunky wasted no time in conjecture. We stowed the schooner foresail, put a double reef in the main and set a storm jib. We had barely finished when a black squall came down on us and we took off like a scalded cat. Visibility was down to a hundred yards. The squall lasted about ten minutes, but it left the mean wind force higher and it was raining solidly. In the next half hour there came two more squalls, each heavier than its predecessor. Chunky sent everybody below leaving just the two of us.

'I don't like this!' Chunky said. 'We'll be running blind. I think we'll heave-to!' We drove on into the roaring murk. If we didn't heave-to we would end up trying to clear Bembridge Ledge on the eastern corner of the Isle of Wight, a tide-swept reef jutting out athwart our course. The succession of squalls, each stronger than its predecessor was a classic feature of mounting heavy weather.

It was now black night and howling. Round she came, and our bows met the sea with a solid crash and an explosion of spray. We were suddenly knocked flat. The stowed staysail wrenched loose with a bellow of flogging canvas. Chunky was yelling something. I began crawling forward. The staysail was climbing the stay. I drew level with the foremast.

The jib sheet parted with a crack and instantly, above my head, the pair of wire pendants dissolved into a ball of blue fire. The bulls-eyes, fist sized, whirled in a lethal frenzy welding themselves together. Then the sail burst in a crazy welter of rope, wire and rag. I lay flat. I was so flat that you could have rolled me up like a doormat.

By the time I'd crawled aft and reported to Chunky the wind was blowing in earnest. Despite the blackness there was a pale luminescence. It was impossible to stare to windward, but the face of the sea had become flattened in a solid blast of wind-driven salt, our rigging was howling, and the roar of wind and water was deafening. With only the deep-reefed mainsail on her she kept luffing up, which seemed set to shake the masts out of her. Chunky gave me the wheel and went forward. Moments later he'd eased the peak halyard and scandalised the mainsail, halving its effective area. She paid off a bit and lay six points off the wind, fore-reaching slightly. There was one more surprise in store.

A squall laid us hard over and pinned us there. Some large dark object flew through the air, across the deck between the masts, over the fore-boom and vanished from sight in the blackness. We'd been carrying a ten foot dinghy in davits, but not any more!

The blow continued all night, veered westerly at first light and eased enough for us to set a bit of sail. We'd been fore-reaching all night, heading out into the Channel. We saw a freighter on a northerly heading. We assumed she was making for Southampton so we bore off and followed her.

The companionway doors opened and a face peered out. 'What time is breakfast please?' its owner demanded.

There was a sour sequel to the loss of our dinghy. A few weeks later came notification from (I suppose) the Receiver of Wreck Department that our dinghy had been recovered by French fishermen and taken into Fécamp where it was in the keeping of French Customs. We sailed over to pay the salvage and collect her.

Some Frenchmen have a deep-rooted dislike of the British. Crecy and Trafalgar figure somewhere, and we sensed it when the Douane and his assistant came aboard to clear us. He was large and florid; his breath put you in mind of the back door of a brewery. Swaying, brooking no argument, he ordered a search of the ship.

His sidekick was plainly embarrassed, working his eyebrows up and down like a shop-window Father Christmas. The cabin sole must be taken up, thundered his boss between hiccoughs. Chunky went steely-grey. 'Non!'

We were suspected of smuggling *women*! What sort, colour, race or creed was not made clear. The matter was resolved by giving the officer a whacking tot of scotch that put him out like Fairy Tinkabell's little light. It made him a hand-cart job.

We never got our dinghy. After its seventy-mile drift it was scoured bare of varnish, oars, boards, or anything movable. The fisherman, gobbling with greed, demanded a sum so absurd that a new boat would have been, and was, cheaper.

Chunky Duff was in no sense a yachtsman. Not for him the club tie, three cheers for the Commodore and a harbour stow. He had been in his element amongst the tunny fishermen, and the scruffier things looked on deck the better. I suppose it was cocking a snoot at the Establishment. At one stage he seriously considered running cargoes of new potatoes from Jersey.

The fact that *Hoshi* was a 'gentleman's yacht' of Edwardian vintage rated for nothing. In Chunky's eyes she was a working boat and there was nothing to choose between the transport of spuds and lodgers. Accordingly some drastic changes were made to the old yacht during the winter of 1947.

She was slipped and her lead ballast keel was removed. Her mainsail was fitted with brails, Thames-barge fashion. I lived aboard, and, whenever the weather permitted, I squatted on a raft alongside, burned and scraped her down to bare wood (mahogany!), then coated her with hot black varnish – a refined coal tar and a total desecration, as unthinkable as Michelangelo painting-by-numbers.

Between times I transferred granite ballast kerbstones by the dinghy-load, swaying them aboard by the Spanish burton which I had rigged, and lowering them into her bilges. To have dropped just one of them would have sunk her.

After a trial sail Chunky declared himself satisfied with her trim and general stiffness. He nominated me skipper and, financed by the lead keel, set about building up his surveying business. He produced a mate for me.

Sam came aboard with a small cardboard suitcase. He was wearing what was known then as 'full drape': a 'teddy-boy' mid-thigh coat with velvet collar, a duck's-arse haircut with Elvis forelock, stovepipe pants and winkle-pickers. I gulped hard. He said 'Wotcher'.

Sam had no knowledge of boats, but he knew a bit about engines and he had his sea-legs, or rather 'dodge-em' legs. His previous job had been with a travelling funfair, collecting money on the rides. I'd seen them: there's the ride, roaring and rattling around with all the birds squealing, and there's your fare collector swaying, dead-pan, debonair, mocking danger, making change.

The first bunch was, of all things, a charter party who described themselves as 'a yachting family from Hendon' which sounded like a limerick rhyming Hendon with 'catch you bend'n' – which they did. There was Sir, a strutting, clockwork little man, and Ma'am, so heavily corseted that she looked as if she was wearing a barrel. There were also a pale son and daughter in their late teens.

Ma'am assumed that Sam would cook. She unpacked a bag containing beef, spuds, carrots and Brussels sprouts.

'Will you look at this,' she said.

Sam looked. 'Them's sprouts!' he identified, nobody's fool. Then he disappeared aloft to grease something.

We sailed on Sunday, so that meant Sunday lunch. We had an hour or more of calm water before we crossed Chichester bar and reached the sea. The meal was just about ready by the time we got to the Nab, and we were chucking about a bit. There were tight lips and parchment faces all around. The table was gimballed, which means that as she rolls, your plate rises and falls between chin and lap, and if you make a grab for it the effect is explosive. Somebody did ... we found a mummified sprout behind a settee months later.

So it was head-down-bum-up all along the lee rail, and I bore off for Sandown Bay where there was shelter of sorts. They slept until evening, then announced that they'd go ashore to dine.

The shelter was minimal. The holding ground was appalling, being pebbles which is about as lethal as polished parquet to high heels. I explained this.

'You won't be more than an hour will you?' I said. 'If the wind backs a bit we'll have to get out of here!' I told Sam to put them ashore on the pier by dinghy. 'Op in the boat and I'll row yer,' he invited graciously.

'Don't you mean I'll row *Sir?*' Ma'am said.

'Yus, 'im an all,' Sam told her.

Predictably, by nightfall the anchorage was untenable, and we were paying out chain like a Special Offer, engine half ahead and cursing ourselves hoarse. Sam laid off in wait, and we eventually got them aboard in frosty silence.

I said we were getting under way at once and hands to the anchor windlass please. They all went to bed, leaving us to tackle sixty fathoms of stud-link on our own. On our route back to the Solent I hunted out every rip, overfall and tide race shown on the chart. They were rattling around in their bunks like Mexican beans.

Round at Yarmouth it happened again. Sir confronted Sam with a dog whistle and blew it. 'We are going ashore to dine,' he said. 'When you hear that (he blew it again), bring the boat ashore for us!'

'Not easy,' Sam said. 'We'll be ashore in the boozer.'

The Shingles Buoy fracas didn't help either.

We were tacking out through the Needles Channel, which is flanked to the north by the shallow Shingles bank. You go about in good time because you can't afford to miss stays – not drawing nine foot you can't. Sir was on the helm, Sam was on jib sheets and I was heaving the leadline. I took a shot.

'Put her round!'

Nothing happened. Sir had his lower lip stuck out.

'Tack NOW!'

'I'll tack when I judge that it is time to tack!' he sulked.

I nodded to Sam who seized the wheel and buzzed it around. Brrrrrrrrrrrrrrr went Sir's knuckles.

But the thing that eventually blew it and ended in solicitor's letters was the tail-shaft incident. We were under power when this drumming noise started. The after end of the engine and the tail-shaft protruded aft into the large cabin occupied by Ma'am and Sir. We needed to see.

Sam had his hand on the cabin door. How were we to know that the old bat was in residence? He said, ringingly, 'Let's have a look at the old girl's tail-shaft; she probably needs her stuffing gland tightened up!' He booted the door open.

There she sat at her dressing table in her pink barrel and gigantic bloomers. She looked like a member of the Papal Guard.

The rest of the season was trauma-free, then came the mussel soup drama. We had a party consisting of two pairs of whispering couples, a jovial ex-sports editor, and a jovial, very large lady. It was messy weather, and we dashed from shelter to shelter as one low followed another. It was church fête weather. Vicars everywhere were agreeing that there were poor souls in the Sudan praying for rain, while serving out soggy quiche on sagging paper plates.

We ended up stuck in Cherbourg waiting for a weather window for a cross-Channel dash for home. Our punters were broke, but they had enough francs left for a last lunch ashore provided it was basic, like mussel soup.

'There looks to be a bit of a gap coming,' I announced, 'We may sail this evening.'

Off they went while we got busy, pulling down reefs in all directions and lashing everything lashable. They came back in good time, and we sailed. The wind was offshore offering a port quartering run; clouds whipped low overhead like torn paper bags. Outside the breakwater the mainsail filled with a bang, and away we went.

'Maybe a nice drop o' Bovril would cheer 'em up!' Sam hazarded, sticking his head down the hatch and saying so. There was silence below save for a shuddering groan.

We settled down to share the night between us. The wheel work was lively; we rode the surges in bursts of phosphorescence, rigging soughing and sighing. We were vaguely aware of the loo pump clattering away down below almost continually. We hadn't heard about the mussel soup.

At about two in the morning I decided to nip below and make some tea. The companionway stairs were amidships abaft the main-mast, debouching upon an area running the width of the ship, with the loo to port and a cabin to starboard. This piece of geography is important to the astonishing scene about to unfold.

I was no ballctomane with a little bead evening bag and powdered shoulders. I would have considered a *tour en l'air* to be a Thompsons package to Ibiza, but I could appreciate a nice spot of choreography when I saw it! There was a heavy roll to starboard. I heard a muffled feminine expletive from the loo, whereupon the door burst open and out bounded our buxom lady!

I watched entranced as, *shackled around her ankles*, she hop-hop-hopped, bringing up all-standing against the opposite side, just as the reverse roll began. I was just a simple sailing lad and unused to exotica. Still shackled by fetters of pink crêpe de Chine she *bounded backwards* into the loo again and the door slammed shut behind her. There was a sickening crash of shattered porcelain and a vile epithet.

I realise now, with the wisdom of hindsight, that I was unwise to have offered my services with the Elastoplast.

The smashing of the loo pan proved an unparalleled disaster for the other mussel soup sufferers who, to put it as delicately as I can, were afflicted in both fantail and fo'c'sle. There was an instant demand for buckets. But the night's drama was not yet over.

Dawn was breaking, or attempting to, if a gradual dilution of murk by an addition of muddy water can be termed 'dawn'. We saw our retired sports editor come on deck and totter uncertainly to the rail clutching his bucket. We averted our gazes squeamishly. Suddenly he let out a yell.

He was flat on his face and being drawn overboard under the guardrail, one arm extended, bucket lanyard around his wrist. Sam grabbed him but lost the bucket. The old gent lay there panting and badly shaken by the experience, then he got his breath back.

'Supposing,' he said, 'just supposing that you'd had to write to my wife to tell her that the last you saw of old George, he was in mid-Channel hanging on to a bucket of crap!' To which he added philosophically, 'She'd have believed you.'

11

A nice apple drink • All gone • A star to steer by • Love on a buoy • A fine exhibition of seamanship

Hoshi, launched in 1906 for the son of Earl Jellico, had been an Edwardian toy. A white yacht: topsides like bone china, teak decks bleached and scrubbed snowy, and sails a dazzle of white on spars pale as peeled willow. She had followed the regattas from Great Yarmouth around the south coast to Torbay cruised by her crew, while her owner came in comfort by road or rail.

The war years had dulled her beauty, and now we had reduced her to a drab. Chunky wanted it thus: 'yachtiness' was to be avoided at all cost. The more she resembled a fishing smack the better. We had tarred her, shorn her of her keel, rigged her like a barge with a brailed mainsail and allowed her varnish brightwork to blacken and flake. No warps were cheesed down, no sails were given 'harbour stows' and her brass became green for want of polishing. My admiration for Chunky was such that I saw nothing whatsoever amiss in this.

The brailed mainsail was intended to make sail handling simpler. The gaff remained aloft and the sail was loose-footed. There were three brails – peak, throat and lower – which, when pulled, gathered in the skirts of the sail against the mast and the underside of the gaff. The snags were that the set of the sail was spoiled by the weight of the brails hooking the leech of the sail, and, when brailing up with the wind from abaft the beam, you got great swollen bundles like some nightmare bag wash.

The windage thus caused meant that when anchored in strong wind-against-current conditions she was apt to 'sail' all over the anchorage, bringing up with tremendous yanks then zooming off again. The skippers of nearby anchored yachts regarded us without love. You'd see portholes framing angry little faces like some sort of aquarium. Lash the wheel how we might or let go the kedge underfoot, it availed us nothing.

Hoshi *under her brailing mainsail rig which gave it the familiar night-watchman's trouser appearance. The flax foresail set like a hammock. By comparison a moth newly hatched from its chrysalis was well dressed.*

In later years and with decent sails, she regained some of her pre-war Edwardian grace. I had long since moved on.

The climax came when our bowsprit probed the fore-triangle of a plump little two-tonner. It was like a cocktail stick spearing a canapé. There was room for an olive and a knob of cheese.

'We're only here for the night!' grieved a little man with a chin-fringe – what the hell difference that made was hard to see. We had to wait for the next tide-turn to get shut of him.

Sam had turned into a valuable hand by now. His full drape, winkle-pickers and stovepipe trousers had become salt-impregnated and much mellowed, and he had developed a taste for sea-going, which was just as well because the lodgers we were getting were pig-ignorant of it.

We had a party of eight footballers from the Midlands, one of whom stuck his boot straight through the saloon skylight the minute he got on board and later crowned this achievement by puking into my seaboot stockings which were hanging up to dry on the boom-gallows. We got all kinds of people.

On one cross-Channel cruise we had a little old lady. She looked so frail that you expected her to shatter like an ornament. A rug over her knees and a little bit of knitting seemed her mark. She told me, confidingly, that going to sea under sail was her lifelong dream. Her father had been a sailor and her four brothers had gone to sea while she had stayed home and bottled plums.

'Sod that!' she said startlingly.

I was scared stiff watching her totter around on deck, staring aloft, helping to heave on ropes, but what could we do except teach her to steer a compass course where she'd at least be safe and the hell with our erratic wake.

At least, I thought, hopefully she'd be content to stay in her bunk for the night crossing. Oh no. She cornered me saying, 'The one thing I've always longed to do ever since I read that poem about a tall ship and a star to steer by is to do just that!'

So once it was good and dark I put her on the wheel, showed her the course and then found her a star to dance on the fore weather crosstree and let her get on with it, picking another star when that one failed to match the compass heading. She sat there, hour after hour, refusing to be relieved, a little old dear singing to herself very softly, gazing up with her eyes shining to match any star, hands passing the spokes to and fro, entranced. At last, when she fell asleep across the wheel, we put her to bed. She left us all sharing her enchantment.

W e had a couple of months of trouble-free cruising, learning to work as a team, especially when anchoring. Sam's job was forward. We were trying to anchor outside Yarmouth, Isle of Wight, west of the pier and there wasn't a lot of room, I gave Sam a thumbs-up; he had the Nicolson hanging outside the bow fairlead, and he pulled the chain brake off. We fell astern, Sam paying out cable. We picked up sternway and more cable ran out. We fell astern, drifting fast to leeward beam-on. Astern lay the pier, and a little cruiser with her owner making twittering noises. An awful suspicion dawned, and I raced forward and looked down at our stem. Like an acrobat the anchor was hanging by one fluke from the bobstay.

After that I devised a system: I would sing out 'Let go', or I would blow a whistle, and Sam would check before yelling 'All gone'. What could possibly go wrong? My naivety is one of my charms.

We had a crowd of total greenhorns, Cherbourg first stop. In the pre-marina days you berthed stern-to in the Avant Port, which meant that the anchor had to be positioned very accurately in mid-basin, then you sent a warp ashore and hauled her tail in to the wall. With more than sixty feet separating helmsman from anchor it called for careful judgement. My usual routine was to circle the basin under engine and size things up, noting shore marks, and then let go next time round. I had a dinghy swung out in davits with a warp in it ready to be run ashore and two of the brighter lodgers standing by the davit falls. Sam was kneeling by his anchor brake. It should have gone like a clockwork hen.

There was a sudden commotion, blocks squealed, a lodger croaked and there was a splash. The man on the forward fall had let it go by the run. In went the bows of the dinghy which promptly began to fill! The man on the after fall, still holding fast, turned on me a countenance of agonised indecision. 'I cocked it up.'

'LET GO!' I howled, fatally, damningly.

Up forward Sam sprang into action, away went the pick. 'All Gone!' he cried triumphantly, peering over the bow as taught.

We were clipping along at a nice three knots. The anchor brought us up with a crash, the cable streaming aft hard as a rail. She swung in a great arc that took us slam-bang alongside an already moored yacht. Her owner, a military-looking man with a bushy moustache, was not the forgiving sort. He took me apart limb by limb, like a constructional toy.

We sorted out our marbles. With my ears lit up like a hole in a road I motored her round again and this time placed my anchor with precision. The dinghy was lowered smoothly and in got its crew, *both sitting forward and side-by-side*! Like goddam love-birds. It was like watching a nightmare unfold. They windmilled away with their paddles, throwing sheets of spray in every direction, tracing a serpentine course which could have only one possible destination: WHAM, straight into our military neighbour.

What with the spittle and the moustache it took him a little while to find the words. His face changed colour like a chameleon on red flannel.

'By God! Haven't you fools ever been in a boat before?' he howled. My prime prats looked up at him daftly. 'No,' they chorused.

Cherbourg was an eventful destination. There was, for instance, the disturbing case of the 'nice apple drink' or Sam's Revenge.

The party were members of some rigid religious sect; there were eight of them. Their leader took Sam aside.

'Have you found Jesus yet, my friend?' he asked.

'Naw,' says Sam, 'but e's probably darn the fo'c'sle unpacking his gear mate!' It was a poor start.

We got under way heading for Cherbourg. Then came lunch: veal and ham pie, limp lettuce and a slice of cake served by Sam, personalised by his thumbprint. Vincent, their leader, said grace.

'We give Thee thanks Lard Gard for this thy bountiful bit of meat pie and Thy small bit of cake,' he intoned. Sam frowned; the mick was being extracted.

When we got the bottles out and invited them to chip in on the kitty, Vincent raised his hands in horror – the Demon Drink was aboard.

'*I would rather drink hemlock!*' he shuddered.

'No 'emlock mate,' Sam said, 'though we might have a Newcastle Brown.'

It was middling choppy so there was a lot of groaning and praying done. Somebody puked on the warps coiled aft, and Sam, in sluicing them off, managed to soak the sufferer responsible. Relationships were deteriorating. We got in and berthed.

'We'll go ashore for supper,' Vincent said. 'Can you recommend a

healthy fruit drink?' I suggested one. Later I saw Sam buttonholing him. I wish I'd known then what had passed between them.

It was nearly midnight when the police brought them back. There was some blood and a missing tooth, and the cops went on something terrible but since I didn't speak French I had to guess. It seemed that the Argentinian navy was in port on a 'good will' visit. There had been a 'disagreement'; a potted shrub had been used as an offensive weapon. Vincent was keen on the idea of disembowelling Sam.

I had it out with him in private. His spherical face radiated injured innocence. 'All I done was tell 'em abaht this 'ealthy apple drink!'

I should have guessed Sam's idea of a healthy apple-drink. I said, 'It was bloody *Calvados,* wasn't it!'

Then came the cruise that was to jerk my uncertain career on to a new track, largely thanks to Sam and his propensity for sleep. We had a party of mid to elderly gents, the sort you see on golf courses with suntanned bald heads and a bowel fetish. We got as far as Chichester bar in a rising gale and anchored under the lee of East Head. We were to be there for three days. Sam and I were happy enough down below in the fo'c'sle, overhauling gear while the wind howled overhead, but the old gents were restless. They worked out how many circuits of the deck added up to one statute mile and round and round they went, tramp, tramp, tramp, for hours at a time all breathing deeply and working their elbows.

One of Sam's regular jobs was to light the boiler in the galley which provided hot water for morning ablutions. It held around five gallons, and under it was a six-wick paraffin Bluett heater. The drill was to light it, wait ten minutes for it to heat up, and then turn the wicks down low.

Sam could sleep on a five-barred gate. I had a lot of trouble with him on watch at night – he'd get his chin lodged between a couple of spokes, forty degrees off-course and start snoring like a pipe band. He decided that ten minutes could most profitably be spent 'avin'a little lay dahn mate'.

Meanwhile I was aft turning off the generator and testing the battery. Maybe it was the sudden silence that woke Sam ... in which case our guardian angels were on overtime again. There was a lot of yelling.

'Fire, fire!' came the dreaded and increasingly familiar cry.

I dashed forward. There was a sailcloth curtain dividing the galley from the fo'c'sle, and it was in flames; the paint on the bulkhead and deckhead was bubbling. The heater, left unattended, had boiled over and brewed up!

I have been involved in four boat fires, all potentially dangerous but all ending in farce. It was Widow Twankey time.

Battling past the old gents who were bumping into one another and advising each other to 'Keep Calm', I reached the big extinguisher on the galley bulkhead. 'Bang knob sharply on floor', advised the instructions. I did so and let fly.

Sam, meanwhile, using his initiative (always a pity), had shot up the forehatch, gone pounding aft, down the companionway where he grabbed the other extinguisher off the bulkhead, and back forward along the deck to the forehatch ready to save the day.

'Ere yer are then!' he cried, sticking his great mug down the hatch. Having extinguished the fire, my appliance wouldn't stop, it

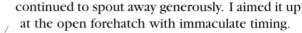

continued to spout away generously. I aimed it up at the open forehatch with immaculate timing.

Next day the wind had eased right off so we got under way. Ordinarily, with half the week gone, I would have stuck to the Solent, taken in Cowes, Beaulieu River and so on, but, after our lamentable exhibition as fire-fighters, I felt that I was conscience-bound to make a bit of effort. We took *Hoshi* south-about around the island, in a real old tumble of leftover sea, and on to Poole Harbour where I stuck her alongside the quay so that our party could march up and down while deep breathing.

Poole Harbour held bitter memories of thwarted passion for me. Once upon a time it was a flying boat base, and the huge circular rubber-edged mooring buoys still remained, a boon to visiting yachtsmen, especially with wind against tide since a boat could bump away at the buoy without damage. If you wanted an undisturbed night – and, by heaven, I did! – that was the place to moor.

I had chartered a little old cruiser with an evil and devious plan of seducing a cooperative girlfriend. She was nothing of a sailor, but then neither was she Little Miss Muffet.

It was doomed from the beginning: drizzle, failing breeze, an engine that packed up, and the full ebb out of Poole Harbour. She was queasy, chilly, and radiating trouble. I tried to cheer her by pointing out various educational sights such as a row of shags and Portland Bill. 'Ever so nice, I'm sure!' she said gratingly.

'Once we're on a mooring all will be saved,' I thought. I had invested lavishly in a tinned pudding, a bottle of VP port, and another of cherry brandy to kick-start the seduction. There would be lamp-light, eyes would meet across the table ...

The mooring ring was in the centre of the buoy and out of reach unless you jumped aboard it. I inched us up-tide until our topsides were nuzzling the buoy. I explained the workings of tiller, throttle and gear lever to my fair companion.

'If she starts to drop back just give her the teeniest touch of throttle,' I explained soothingly. I took the rope and clambered onto the buoy.

The stupid bitch banged the throttle open wide. There I was, crouching like a frog on a lily pad bellowing while she went

zooming past. Right round she went, then straight at me. I took a flying leap as she roared past. Then I blew it; wasted was the planning, the VP port and the tinned pud. 'You bloody stupid cow!' I screamed. I spent the night on a sagging pipecot in the forepeak. Next morning she caught the first train home.

Now, years later, with our gentlemen charterers, we left Poole Quay homeward bound, and, with a light head wind and a strong fair tide under us, we headed down the winding channel through the moorings for the harbour entrance. The old gentlemen were at harbour stations solidly blocking the helmsman's view. All was quite normal.

We were nearing the end of the moorings; relatively open water and the narrows at the entrance lay ahead. Suddenly the engine note changed to that dreaded adenoidal tone which meant that the cooling water was running dry and that if I didn't shut it off the engine would seize up. Being head-to-wind we hadn't set any sail. It was the moment for me to execute a brilliant bit of seamanship.

But I didn't.

What I *should* have done was round her up, cut the engine and stem the tide. Her bare windage would then have provided me with steerage against the current. Then, by setting a little sail, I could have reached a clear patch of water and anchored. What I *did do* was pay off to port, let go the brails and set the mainsail while Sam struggled with the foresail and jib.

We lay closehauled athwart the current, moving sluggishly ahead and smartly beam-on down-tide. It was a course designed for a sorry conclusion. We sagged down through the moored yachts missing them by miraculous inches. An owner bobbed up through a hatch with his face lathered with shaving soap, mouth open like a clown. He wasn't laughing. Ahead of us and a mite down-tide were the fateful flying boat moorings and moored to each one was a large glossy powerboat, all glass and chromium but ('thank thee Lord') nobody aboard. It went like this:

I gripped the spokes, white-knuckled, groaning 'O God, thousands of quids-worth of damage!' With the wheel hard up we slid inexorably forward to disaster. We shaved down-tide of the first yacht. The next lay ahead and to port. Our bow hit the circular buoy and *we rolled along it with our bilge*. Then our bows cocked downstream as our stern rolled clear. We sailed another length. A third large gin palace loomed. Our bowsprit missed her wheelhouse, missed the launch in davits and, neat as plucking a lily, snapped off her ensign staff. Sam, reading the runes, was already casting off the anchor lashing and humping it over the rail. 'LET GO!' I squealed, and away it went. We brought up with a jarring crash and swung. We brailed up and clawed down foresail and jib. I gave vent to a deep and shuddering sigh. Then an extraordinary thing happened. One of those elderly gents, deep breathing, bowel-regular, corn-fed and marvellous-for-his-age, fixed me with his eye and said, 'I never saw such an exhibition!'

I stood there, head bowed, waiting to be withered like a salted slug.

'Congratulations skipper,' he added, 'on a magnificent piece of seamanship!'

I thought he was taking the piss, but far from it. At the end of the cruise he took me aside and offered me a job as a seamanship instructor with the Outward Bound Sea School. He was one of the Trustees. He said my talents would be fully stretched ... a worthwhile job ... career prospects ... I needed career prospects like a Bedouin needs his camel.

Clean thoughts and cold showers • Lower-and-dip • Wedded • Shepherd o' the hills

The Outward Bound Sea School in Aberdovey, Wales, was founded in wartime to teach Merchant Navy cadets how to stand up to the rigours of ships sunk by U-boat attack and to cope with lifeboat survival. It had a motto: *To serve, to strive but not to yield*.

So the lads puffed up mountains, paddled canoes, heaved their guts out on the sweeps of cutters and vomited therapeutically at the lee rail of the school ketch. They took cold showers and renounced smoking, girls and foul language – which left most of them struck dumb.

They did a one-month course, and they came from public schools, borstals, industry and private homes. Nationalities were mixed and so was the staff. The overall influence was Merchant Navy plus an overlay of running-on-the-spot, knees-bend, physical fitness gurus. I was billeted next door to Stan Hugill, a one-time Cape Horner and the last British sailor to be signed on a four-masted barque as AB Shantyman – he was to become a world authority on the sea shanty.

Winter mornings, when shivering lads had to unlash frozen ties and clamp scarlet hands around frozen oar looms, were particularly rich in character-moulding – something sorely lacking in some of those croaking little morons. You'd get lads from industry, reared on trade union dogma, waxing wrath about strenuous activity. 'You done this back in't factory, you'd have em all out – sir!' they'd gripe.

'Shut up and clap on!'

The dipping-lug rig of the cutters was totally labour intensive when tacking. On the command 'Lower-and-dip', the helm was put down, the halyard (the mast was unstayed) was slacked away, unhooked, carried forward around the bow and rehooked on the new weather side, while the tack of the sail was unhooked, passed around the foot of the mast and rehooked to leeward, whereupon the halyard was swigged up and the sheet hauled aft. You ended up with a huge canvas parcel of cursing adolescents while the remainder acted as movable ballast ... which was almost my undoing.

On my first day in a cutter I had a crew of absolute novices with the dead eyes of the totally disinterested. I spelled it out to them in simple one-syllable words. 'This is the *WEATHER* side', I enunciated carefully, thumping it by way of identification. 'It is called that because it is the side *upon which the wind is blowing*, OK?' They yawned and studied the scenery.

'And this is the *LEE* side because it is *down-wind*, got it?' Their eyes ranged the estuary; one whistled a little tune. I gritted my teeth and ploughed on.

'At all times, AT ALL TIMES, your body weight must be *ON THE WEATHER SIDE*!' What could be plainer than that?

Off we sailed; they were all lined up along the weather side nice as you like. Then we tried a tack.

The storming of the Bastille was a fun-run by comparison. Sails flogged, ropes cracked, lads cursed. 'All up to windward, WEATHER SIDE, lads!' I shrilled as we came through the wind. They knew where the weather side was. They'd *been* there. They went there again. It was doubly instructional – they learned how life jackets worked.

The underlying aim of the OBSS was character building. Between exertions on mountain and sea, by way of cold showers and lee rail, you found what a lad had in him: usually no more than breakfast. There were occasional miracles.

Lads were divided into 'watches' of fourteen boys, which elected and demoted their own leaders with much angry croaking. Watches competed for the watch trophy. Competition could be awesome.

The social mix, too, could be explosive. You got Adrian from Virginia Water with his pigskin suitcase and mellifluous accent bunking next to Mac from the Gorbals who owned neither suit nor case. Eyes were blackened and noses thumped. There was a jet black Gold Coaster lumped in alongside a latter day leftover from Hitler Youth who howled racial superiority and started World War III. By the end of the month they were staunch buddies, and they had whipped their apathetic watchmates into a winning team.

There was a heart-warming case involving a loutish bully reduced to jelly by his victims. The twenty mile Cader Idris trek was a trial of endurance. Lads went off in groups of five, and it was rough. We, the instructors, had the chilly job of sitting, on mountain tops to check them through.

Lads. Cold showers, clean thoughts and regular vomiting provided a healthy environment that made men of them and emotional wrecks of instructors.

They were supposed to stay together, but four lads set their jaws, forced the pace, and literally walked their tormentor into the ground. We looked the other way.

'Waaait!' he blubbered, falling further and further behind.

Then there was a mummy's boy scared to tackle the (voluntary) aerial 'death slide' between two trees and spanning a valley. Again and again he chickened out while the others whooped down gleefully. Then it became serious; some chemistry took place, and, without a word, the other kids melted out of sight into the bushes. Scattering tears like a crop sprayer *he did it!* There was a roar of applause for an ex-wimp suddenly ten feet tall. Mum was due for a surprise.

But then there was 'Shrimp' who spat, stole, smoked and peed behind the watch hut, a vile little toad and filthy with it.

It was midwinter, and when his watch did their trip in the ketch they hit bad weather. The skipper, an ex-Tasmanian hardcase considered that the place to be was hove-to with plenty of searoom well offshore, not hugging an anchor. It was my turn for ketch duty. Well it would be, wouldn't it.

We lay hove-to somewhere in St George's Channel, lurching and

81

Warspite *Outward Bound Sea School Aberdovy.* Ex-Bluebird *that caught fire off the Manacle Buoy and aboard which I used my initiative. Which was a pity.*

rolling, blasted by snow flurries. We two mates shared the watches, huddled in the deckhouse between deck rounds. The boys each did a half-hour wheel-watch. Snow and vomit, highly therapeutic. The old man kept his carpet slippers on as usual.

Shrimp took it upon himself to do his watch-mate's duties. By the time we discovered this little act of dedication he was rigid with cold.

'Them useless buggers are good fer ****-all,' he explained, in morse code, through chattering teeth. Hero of the day he was praised and cosseted by all. But, once ashore again, he reverted to form, loathed by all.

I caught another twisted little no-hoper smoking in the loo. He said, paraphrasing the school motto, 'I've served and strived, now I'm bloody yieldin' – sir!'

Noble deeds became addictive. I found a sheep up on the mountain; it was staggering around bleating, plainly in need of succour (or sucker). I shouldered it and started off down to the farm in the valley. It voided bowels and bladder simultaneously and unstintingly.

The farmer leaned over his gate watching. I panted up to him. I said, 'I found this poor sick beast up on the fell; where do you want me to put it?'

OK, so I didn't expect him to fall about sobbing with gratitude; Welsh sheep farmers aren't cut out for it. He spat.

'Where shall you put it, boyo? I'll tell you where to put it. Right back where you bloody found her is where!' Apparently he had dosed her and taken her up there not half an hour earlier. He relented and took us both back up by tractor. He was the richer for having another 'stupid English' anecdote to add to his repertoire.

There was another occasion when we went to sea and hove-to. It was a night to match the Shrimp episode if not nastier; it was a night for something a bit more nourishing than cocoa. Hard drink was frowned upon, although on occasion peppermint was an all-pervading aroma at the school after a chilly day in the cutters.

We anchored under St Tudwal's Island, where the engineer went ashore to buy a bit of stewing steak to make a lobscouse. He came back with bottle-shaped bulges in his side pockets. The lobscouse having been made and consumed we pulled down our reefs and went to sea, leaving an expensive lobscouse wake as the motion took its toll.

Once we had a safe offing we hove-to for the night. It blew hard from the sou'west. It was bitterly cold, and the lads were excused a wheel-watch; it wasn't necessary anyway with a becket on the spokes and a look-out. When the mate came up to relieve me he brought a waft of peppermint and an air of cheer.

'Give us one,' I said. It seemed he'd just eaten the last, the lying toad.

I stopped off at the engineer's bunk on my way down and sniffed carefully. Peppermint and White Horse. I knocked on his door, it opened an inch.

'Bloody chilly up there,' I said, working my eyebrows up and down.

'Aye noo doubt,' he said, a Scot like the mate. He closed the door in my face.

All night we shared the deck watches between us. Each time the mate came on he reeked of peppermint and *made jokes.* I had brick feet.

Then the Old Man came shuffling up into the deckhouse where I sat huddled; he had on his carpet slippers and dressing gown, and

his breath reeked of peppermint. Ho ho, I thought.

He thumped the barometer. 'First rise after low soon foretells a stronger blow,' he mourned with lugubrious satisfaction. Then, having wiped a peephole in the condensation and taken official cognisance of the situation on deck, he shuffled below to his cabin again.

The mate relieved me, and I creaked below shedding permafrost. The Old Man's cabin door opened a fraction. 'Sssst!' he said, jerking his head in invitation. I went in.

'You need a little something to warm you up, lad,' he whispered, 'only we mustn't let the world know, eh!'

'Oo no!' I said.

What would it be? I wondered. Brandy? A nice drop of twelve-year-old malt, maybe? Or was he a ninety-proof rum man?

He produced a brown paper bag. 'Have a bullseye, son.'

I married my sail-locker sweetheart, without fuss, from the home of Bill and Biddy Smart, and powered by Dutch gin. We moved into furnished rooms in Aberdovey near the sea-school. Our landlady, a staunch teetotaller, chapel-goer and humourless bundle of gloom, lived upstairs. There was no honeymoon, but our first Christmas was memorable.

My new father-in-law sent us a chicken far too early. We lacked a fridge. It was ready-plucked, its limbs tied in knots, and God-knows-what stuffed up its stern. It looked like some small-time wrestler who'd tangled with Big Daddy.

'We'll paint it with vinegar,' Joyce explained, calling up a bit of folklore learned at mother's knee. We didn't just paint it; we *soaked* it.

It was to be Joyce's first wedded Christmas dinner. The chicken reeked of vinegar like the local chippy. Clang went the gas oven door. We sat sipping sherry; time passed. The dinger dinged. I followed Joyce to the kitchen, sniffing, filled with foreboding. She opened the oven door.

A suffocating stench of roasting corruption hit us. Joyce fled in tears, wailing, while I set about bagging and binning the whole damn disaster.

I sought her out to comfort and console her and learned that it was all my fault. I have never ceased to marvel at my own culpability and limitless aptitude for evil. We had bacon and eggs.

Now that I had a wife and a life outside the school things changed. I no longer spent my evenings yarning with the lads; instead I was on my bike and scuttling back to the village and to the arms of my love. This was not popular at the school. Fortuitously there came a letter.

It was from John Baylay in Salcombe, South Devon, whom I had met on the charter boat circuit. His letter explained that he was starting a sailing project, I had been *Hoshi*'s skipper, she was to be part of the project, and how about us joining him?

There was no decision to be made.

I accepted and handed in my notice and a month later I lowered-and-dipped my last time. We sent our suite of matching luggage on ahead. It consisted of three large tin boxes inscribed 'Schermuly Distress Rockets' and one had a picture of a moustachioed man in a sou'wester all braced up and ready to discharge one of these merciful missiles. It seemed prophetic.

13

*The Island Cruising Club • Does it rock? •
The Lucozade freak • The Great Biscuit Tin
Mystery • Rummaged, wrecked and
run-down • I squat and become a father*

In the fifties there was a universal urge to get afloat but not enough boats to go around. Chemists, mixing their reeking plastic concoctions, were soon to fuel a boat boom, replacing old Ned and his adze and producing scores of plastic yachts, identical as pork pies and shiny as sanitary ware.

Meanwhile there was the Island Cruising Club, run on the lines of a golf or bowling club that owns its links and rinks which the members pay to use. We had yachts and boats instead.

We had *Provident*, a Brixham sailing trawler, four dinghies, an old Six Metre, sundry odd craft, a launch and an ex-RAF rescue launch as a guardship. She had a door cut in her topsides, enlarged from the hole made by a dinghy that missed stays and ploughed through the rotting plywood. Unique also was the toilet flush-tank to be seen on deck. Passers-by would see the chain dip and hear the clunk and gurgle. They would watch keenly to see who came out.

Most of the fleet was bought on tick and with John's rhetoric, which also persuaded us not to expect any wages 'just until we're on our feet'. During the first two years we ran on credit, parish-rig and pilchards-in-tomato, which Beth, John's wife, bought in bulk.

We sailed *Hoshi* up from Chichester, and the season began.

Our clientele were ninety percent raw beginners. I could usually bank on maybe a couple of people who, if not ex-sailors, were at least practically minded and fast learners. The rest brought fishing rods, opera glasses and golf umbrellas. They wore speckled sand-shoes, bicycle capes and expressions of total incomprehension. 'Will it rock?' asked one. 'What time do we dock in Guernsey?' asked another.

They joined ship on Saturdays, changed into baggy shorts and bobble hats, and strolled up and down the deck thumping masts.

Provident, *a Brixham trawler, stiff as a lighthouse, outward bound from Salcombe with the lot up.*

Sunday mornings were sail-drill time; they learned to hoist and, more importantly, to lower and stow sails, how not to fall overboard, and how to operate a marine toilet. Joyce ran a separate and largely whispered seminar for ladies. '*Put nothing down that has not been eaten!*' she would hiss sideways, with emphasis, girl-to-girl.

There were around eighteen ropes to pull in order to set all plain sail, and I would work through them routinely. 'Peak and throat, peak and throat purchases, topping-lift, topsail halyard, topsail tack tackle,' I would intone, indicating each with languid hand like an air hostess indicating escape routes. 'Tickle Topsy's tail,' they would chant hopefully.

Then came this clever Dick with an idea. Instead of everybody trying to learn the lot, why not just learn two or three ropes each? I guessed that if they didn't try it I'd be blamed for every future cock-up from fire and famine to the bloody flux. I went below. I could hear sails going up and down smooth and easy. When I went on deck all was stowed and proper.

'I'm main throat halyard,' said a little man proudly, nodding his bobble at me. 'I'm that thingummy tackle,' said another more vaguely.

We had lunch, set the mainsail and jib, swung her, slipped the mooring and headed down-harbour. 'Up foresail,' I commanded (schooner gaff foresail).

The throat began jerking aloft but the gaff peak dangled like a broken wing. 'Come on, up peak!'

Nothing happened; the throat was now swigged up two-blocks, halyard belayed, coil hitched and hung. The operator beamed, awaiting praise.

'Where's that bloody peak?' I snarled.

There was an uneasy silence. Then a voice said, 'Peak halyard's in't toilet.'

M ainly we cruised the Brittany coasts after a call in the Channel Isles to stock up with cheap booze and tobacco. Once over the bar outward bound we vanished, a gaff-rigged space shot, powered by pilchards in tomato sauce. It was all very casual: just me, Joyce and eight total beginners. In those days we had no life jackets, harnesses, life rafts, pulpits or radios. Our sole concession to safety was a rocket on a six-foot stick. It was probably thirty years old.

Good seamanship was the nub of all operations. Sails were stowed like furled umbrellas, ropes coiled, boats rowed, heaving lines heaved and halyards belayed in seamanlike fashion. A multitude of fancy Turk's heads, coach-whipping and stopper knots sprouted everywhere like some rare fungus. Nobody *ever* referred to 'behind' instead of 'abaft'.

Everybody steered, including those who did so in great sweeping curves as if icing a cake. No matter how gruesome they felt they were turned out for their watch, even if they were sent back to their bunks ten minutes afterwards. It meant they'd be able to hold their heads up later – advisable since they'd be booming into a bucket. Also those who made the effort to turn out unprompted could regard their horizontal shipmates with smug compassion.

I found that it was better not to start howling and yelling until things demanded a maximum exertion, whereupon the indignation and resentment engendered released an explosion of adrenaline, the thistle under the tail. A good discharge of adrenaline has the power of a forklift truck.

Seasickness afflicted about sixty percent of crew. Most bore it stoically; some played it for all it was worth with resonant groaning,

Joyce, my long-suffering wife, aboard Provident *and queen of* Hoshi's *foredeck, galley and sail-locker. She kept me cheerful. 'Stop that!' she'd rasp.*

rolling eye and calls upon their Maker. There was a young engaged couple; he honked his way to Guernsey powered by a single Cream Cracker. 'That bloody does it!' the girl said. 'Imagine *that* across the breakfast table for a lifetime. No THANK YOU!'

Experts tell us that there is no complete immunity to motion-sickness; somewhere there is a motion which will turn you butt up and head down. One visualises the researcher with clipboard and sick-bag moving pessimistically from sedan chair to big dipper. Now and then you got one who was genuinely ill and cause for concern, or, like little Billy, who reacted bizarrely. While it was not a subject to be joked about the 'banana-skin' aspect was not to be dismissed lightly.

We berthed alongside after a lumpy crossing, and Billy went ashore with the rest seeking recuperation on the beach in the sun. He returned with a bottle of Lucozade. He sought me out.

'Take no notice of what they're saying about me!' he whispered hoarsely.

It was about 2am when the racket began, hollering and yelling, doors banging. I quit the sail locker where Joyce and I slept and raced forward. It appeared that Billy had knotted his hanky into a bag, filled it with health-giving Lucozade, and hung it up by his bunk, handy for night nourishment. It *leaked*! His fellow sleepers in the fo'c'sle had plainly stolen it! He played hell.

I peered down the open forehatch. I had a beard of sorts in those days. 'Hello Jesus!' he greeted me affably. 'Jesus wants me for a sunbeam', he sang, beating time to himself.

I bawled him out. He quit his bunk, ripped off his pyjamas, raced up on deck, chucked his wristwatch overboard and leapt into a dinghy that was hanging in davits. This was too much to bear and, drawing a bucket of harbour water, I gave it to him square in the bum.

'Wheeee!' he yelled, demanding more. Then he shot below again and, dripping wet, nipped into somebody else's bunk. Which was when the gravy hit the fan and he socked me; my nose spouted gore.

I decided he had sunstroke. The harbour watchman was staring down from the quay.

'I need a doctor', I informed him.

'So does that bugger!' he said making for his phone.

The duty doctor was down in a flash, and I led him to the forehatch. Billy was now going on about 'The Oxford Group'. The doctor's diagnosis was succinct and to the point: 'Wow!' he said.

He phoned for the police ambulance and six coppers. They came loping down and disposed themselves around the deck, kneeling, squatting, or standing sideways abaft the mainmast and all carrying truncheons.

'He's only a little feller,' I told the rozzer in charge. He took in my gory hooter. 'You could fool me, sir!' he said with fervour.

Billy appeared suddenly, fully dressed, bag packed and in a hurry. 'Come on, come on!' he told the coppers, striding briskly ashore and up the steps. They followed looking silly, and all boarded the ambulance. As it drove off I could hear all hell breaking loose.

I phoned the hospital and the matron told me the usual stuff about the patient being 'comfortable' and 'responding to treatment'. She said he was keen to continue his sailing holiday. I told her, 'no way dare I have him back!'

It seemed a good time to go to sea and get the hell out of it. We watered, fuelled and provisioned at high speed. We were all singled up and engine ticking over when a Morris 1000 came squealing along the quay. Out got a large lady built like a Turkish wrestler with a moustache to match. She was wearing a nurse's uniform.

Without preamble she said, 'We've got a wee manny in our care. Well, you'll be glad to hear that he's all fit again and raring to rejoin you!'

I raised a wary hand. 'I'm not sure ...'

'Oh yes,' she said, 'he's as right as rain. Why, d'you know it's the first time I've been kissed in forty years!'

'Let go forr'rd. Let go aft!' I gabbled.

Odd things happen at sea. The biscuit tin was very odd indeed. There is an area of sea southwest of Guernsey, between the island and the Brittany coast, which is *different*; the sea feels different, and there are magnetic anomalies, seabed lodes of iron ore which tug at a compass card with a ghostly hand.

Along the forty-mile route lie the great reefs of Roches Douvres and Barnouic with their sentinel lighthouse. Could magnetic anomaly alone have caused the eerie happening?

We had found a tin of lifeboat biscuits behind the saloon panelling while fitting out. It was long lost and, by its appearance, many, many years old. It had an Edwardian appearance in an Edwardian yacht.

The lid was soldered on, and we mangled it distinctively in getting it off. The contents were like dog biscuits and quite fresh, the sort that breeders recommend for boundless energy and a glossy coat. They neither tasted, smelt nor looked like anything at all; they were totally flavourless and, for this reason, ideal nourishment for the queasy.

The contents had lasted all season. Sufferers not so much nibbled as *eroded* them. Yet, sooner or later, this precious yet non-renewable supply had to end, and it did so as we were sailing from Guernsey towards and to the west of the Roches Douvres.

It was a warm, calm, hazy day, and we were rolling along at four knots with a following breeze. I took the empty tin, set the lid upright in it like a sail and carefully dropped it overboard. In foggy-hazy weather you can judge the range of visibility by watching some floating object disappear astern. I guessed about half a cable (100 yards).

In the Fifties, yacht navigation meant compass, log, lead and look-out; there were no wonder electronics. In fog, you calculated tidal set and drift with great care, made allowance for leeway and the helmsman's skill or lack of it, and came up with a d.r or 'deduced reckoning' or *guess*. Accordingly, I impressed upon successive helms-men and women the need for great concentration. I described the hidden reefs and treacherous currents ahead. You could hear their heavy breathing. They would dine out on it for years.

The day wore on. We never deviated from our course. The wind direction remained constant and so did our speed. The fog eddied and swirled softly. At about three in the afternoon, with another twelve miles distance run on the patent log, our look-out forward reported a ship ahead.

No, not a ship, smaller, a buoy.

No, not a buoy, something yet smaller than a buoy.

A *tin* box. A tin biscuit box with its lid stuck upright, mangled in a distinctive and unmistakable manner.

We passed it just out of boathook reach and we watched it as it fell astern for the second time.

How was it possible? We would have had to sail in a complete circle; that would have meant that the wind would have had to follow us in a circle! Or could another yacht have left an obsolete biscuit tin with it's lid upright on the same day, in the same area ... Or was it a time warp? I shall never know.

Now and again we took *Provident* rather than *Hoshi*. Like most working craft a Brixham sailing trawler is a functional delight. Fishermen were concerned with catching fish rather than weasling out an extra quarter knot or getting a couple of degrees closer to the wind. They wanted a stable working platform that could stay at sea in a winter gale and make a fast passage back to market. When not fishing crew liked to get below, work up a fug, and let the lad sail the ship.

For us there was one sorry Easter cruise, however.

I never liked Easter and Whit weekend cruises: the weather could be turbulent, you had only four days, yet the punter expected to go foreign. If you didn't do so you got lower lips stuck out a doorstep, sighs and mutters.

This occasion was typical; we were stuck in harbour for the first twenty-four hours while it blew a hoolie. Nobody wanted to learn knots down below, and life ran from forecast to forecast.

Other yachts ventured out whereupon everybody became querulous. Why can't we, eh? Tell me that!'

There was one member of crew who got well up my nose from the moment he came aboard. He knew everything about everything to do with the sea and sailing. So, OK, he sat the wrong way round in the dinghy, and his cap looked suspiciously like ex-Fire Service, but then there was lots of odd ex-service kit about.

Harold, for that was his name, knew how to tie knots, he could tell you the international code flags for 'I am on fire', and the rights of way for taxiing seaplanes. He was an easy man to hate.

He said, nasally, 'Correct me but I'd have thought a Brixham trawler could have stood a bit of a blow!'

I saw a weather-window and we went for it. A quick dash across to the Channel Isles, fast and brutish, two hundred Duty Free cigarettes and a bottle of Bucktrouts would shut them up. Harold strode around making out that he was well used to the motion. He banged rigging critically, his expert eye determining whether it was set up right. He had a pair of huge ex-Armoured Corps binoculars around his miserable scrawny neck. If he fell overboard, I reflected pleasurably, they'd take him down like a diving gannet.

We were about halfway across; it was night, and we were

reaching along with a great boil of a bow wave. The chip of a moon dodged tatters of cloud. Distributed along the lee rail were the taut and straining rumps of the suffering.

CRASH! The weather-guy of the bowsprit shroud parted and the spar broke clean at the stemhead. It swept aft taking the port crosstree arm with it and ending up alongside with a mighty thudding and bumping under our bilge. There was a lot of yelling. Harold demanded that the engine should be started, that distress rockets be fired, and a lifeboat summoned. The lee rail jockeys redoubled their threnody of woe, and there was much dashing around.

We weathered the staysail and hove her to. We had to get that twenty feet of battering ram secured before it holed us, which meant a parbuckling job. The parbuckling was dangerous and difficult. With the trawler now corkscrewing around, passing lines between spar and hull, then up-and-over, threatened to reduce our arms to meat paste. Our wives clung on to the backs of our pants, opening a handy gap for deluges of water. I got a fleeting glimpse of Harold's taut bum at the lee rail. There is always a ray of sunshine to be found.

The hobby-horsing of a vessel when hove-to and the way she slams her tail down can have profound results. Years ago an entire tunny fleet lying hove-to in a winter hurricane in Biscay was lost – the slamming of those long counter sterns shook them to pieces. In our case it siphoned up seawater via the exhaust, which had no water-trap and gave us an engine full of water.

Except that we didn't know it at first. The engine was a big German diesel and a bit of war reparations. The standard starting procedure consisted of a jam jar full of paraffin and a lump of pumice on a wire handle. You dipped the pumice in the jam jar so that it soaked up the oil, and then you lit it, pressed the starter, and rammed this flaming accessory up its chuff, so-to-speak. Ordinarily, and perhaps understandably, the engine sucked in its breath a bit sharply, and 'bang', away she went.

No way. It took about half an hour of charging to get the starter battery up enough for a good turnover each time, then light the flambeau, shove it up ... wow-wow-wow-wow wahhhh. Start again. Dawn's heraldic banners slashed the rearguard of retreating night. Over and over: charge, light up, wow-wow-wow on the starter.

'Sod this,' I said, finally. And at that moment a holy angel named Harry (destined in due course, had he but known it, for Pentonville Prison on account of having two wives and somebody else's money) arrived with hot baked potatoes dripping with butter. He'd also lit the stove, and the saloon was warm and golden with lamplight.

We lay hove-to with a becket on the wheel and swayed with the ship, listening to her old bones creaking comfortably. I counted heads. Four were still on deck. We'd better get them down and bed them with a bucket before the deep chill got to them. 'Where's Harold?' I asked generally, guiltily, remembering those huge bino's.

He was in his bunk groaning in abject terror.

Yes, it was scary if you didn't know what was going on. With every roll to leeward and back the rigging let forth a deep,

We lost our bowsprit and parbuckled it back aboard – a night to remember best forgotten. Note the cock-eyed crosstree.

shuddering moan, the rudder clunked, gear creaked and jangled and waves burst over our bluff weather bow with a rattle of spray.

'Ohhhhh!' quavered poor Harold, the man of books, realising a lifelong dream of going to sea under sail.

We reached back to Brixham fast and smoothly. Harold packed his bag and left. I went ashore to the club to phone news of our plight to John and saw Harold at the bar bending the barman's ear.

Just my chance to cheer the poor chap up, I thought. Redeem his self-respect, we all go through it, and so on. I needn't have worried; whatever Harold was short of it sure as hell wasn't self-respect.

'I told him,' Harold was saying to the po-faced barman, 'I told him straight. In my opinion, I said, you're carrying far, far too much sail. Oh, I told him!'

It was as a result of the colonic irrigation we'd given the engine that I got a chance to go sailing, really sailing. We had *Provident* booked for a three-week cruise to west Brittany; the lack of an engine wouldn't alter that. I had an 80-ton ketch to play with. Also, an unknown crew and the rocks and sluicing tides of Ushant. My guardian angel got on his bike.

Engineless sailing is very different to sailing without *using* the

Laid-back aboard Provident

engine; the knowledge that there is a great black hole where an engine used to be improves your seamanship no end. It also makes you a bit canny. There were no yacht marinas at that time. You either berthed alongside, dried out against a wall, anchored or moored. Each case was dominated by two problems: how do I go about getting under way again and how the hell to *stop*.

I made for destinations I could handle, like Cherbourg where the Petit Rade is easy of access under sail (albeit the shops are a hell of a long pull by dinghy). The Island Cruising Club didn't run to outboard motors; we used the 'WAGYAR' method, i.e. work-your-arms-and-give-your-arse-a-ride. There were lamentations.

We went through Alderney Race backwards, having hit a calm patch. An eddy of the boiling, seething current took us towards Quenard point, which has jagged rocks like some nightmare garden centre. It was a horrible moment; we were all trying to push sails about to coax some wind into them. I had a blotting paper tongue.

Upon reaching St Peter Port, Guernsey, I anchored outside like some plague ship. Skeletal hands, foul with the dreaded buboes waved visitors away.

Then we headed for the north Brittany rivers as usual but with forebodings. I was learning that, whatever you attempt under sail only, you must keep plenty of way on. It is no use reducing sail and pussy-footing about; you have to carry plenty and hope to God you can get it off her in a hurry when the time comes. With a leading wind we entered Pontrieux River, and I anchored halfway up when the wind failed. There was a village reachable by dinghy.

Getting under way should have been simple provided we broke out on port tack. On starboard we would head straight for a rocky shore. With a trawler you don't just spin her about; you have to 'sail' her round in slow-motion. Your toes curl up in your boots like gherkins.

Then, in comes this little yacht and anchors smack on the line we'd be taking.

'I say!' I hailed, 'I haven't got an engine. We'll be paying off across you.' 'Haven't you?' this muffin says. '*We've* got a Volvo!' He really was that thick.

We hauled up to our anchor fast to get a bit of way on her. We hoisted and weathered our jib just as we broke out, then we laid off on port with our bowsprit aimed at his after doghouse window. He gibbered.

I had the wheel up, bearing off to clip under his stern, but, instead of hauling ahead, he *cast off his anchor completely*. We ended up with our bowsprit inside his backstay, him alongside us and everybody hollering. We let go our anchor again. He said, incredibly, accusingly, 'You never had a fender out!'

We covered the hundred-mile beat along the north Brittany coast in two bites, letting the ship sail herself, which, to windward, she did more efficiently. A human is either pinching to stay on course or sailing free. Left to herself the ship follows every variation in wind angle. The practice gave great offence to those who fancied themselves at steering. Huffily they remind you that they won the silver teaspoon for unrated cruisers two years in succession.

Throughout the middle hours the wind fell feeble and the tide turned foul. The trawler rolled and humped about, mugs below clattering, a bottle rolling, chain nips aloft clanking like Marley's ghost. I dozed over the chart table.

Then, in came Bob, a stalwart hand.

'Wopff our poffition?' he mumbled indistinctly. I consulted the chart, did a mental sum and pointed a finger.

'About here. Why?'

'Thaff where my fuffing teeth are!' he said, marking it with a cross.

The tide came fair and the coast began to reel by. Everybody was navigating hard, watching the innumerable church towers create false transits and headlands opening and closing like scissors. It seemed a good time to get my head down. We were coming to the nor'west corner of France and the Ushant region which was a good place to have your wits about you.

Four hours later somebody shook me awake.

'We're coming to the end of the land!' a voice said urgently.

It had an ominous sound: twelfth-century flat earth navigators sailing off into space? 'Fair wind Egbert, all downhill from now on!' I went on deck.

We had the lofty pinnacle of Ile Vierge lighthouse astern, the coast curving away, Ushant crouching like cat to the sou'west. I got busy with the tidal atlas, fixed our position, laid a course for rounding the corner. The usual route is the Le Four channel; then there is the Chenal de la Helle, which has a real cheery ring about it, and, further west, inside Ushant, the wider Fromveur Channel. Through these channels the tides rush at speeds of up to 8–10 knots in places. The west-going stream was just beginning to bite.

The wind was dying. It was a pearly-white day. The coast, the rocks and islands were a soft mouse-grey, and the sea breathed in long Atlantic swells, bright-shining and unrippled. The coast fell away, our speed fell, and the helmsman started banging the useless wheel around. We drifted.

It was very peaceful. Somebody produced tea. Ordinarily we would have started the engine, end of problem. What should I do? kedge? The chart showed a depth of between twenty-five and fifty fathoms. In fast tides a warp of that length strums like a banjo and imposes a massive load on a small kedge. We'd drag. Why not just go sou'west with the ebb and nor'east with the flood, and keep plotting position? Kedge if we had to?

Decision-making over I accepted a chocolate Bourbon. Moments later came a rattle from aloft and the jib sheets jangled. A faint zephyr fanned my cheek. The helm came alive; sheets were hardened. It wasn't much of a breeze, but it might strengthen. It was dead in our teeth. It also blew my carefully made decision. What now? Bear away to port and make for the Le Four channel or starboard towards the open sea and get the hell out it altogether, which was no option at all – out there lay one of the busiest shipping lanes in the world.

My Bourbon biscuit suddenly tasted like a bit of bath mat. Then I saw the sea alongside move. It heaved into a table-sized, glossy up-welling, puckered and polished like old scar tissue ... a '*keld*'. I knew what kelds meant; they form when a fast current flows over an uneven

They call them 'kelds': ominous up-wellings, swirls and hisses that betoken a fast tide and a pending navigational cock-up.

seabed. These up-wellings were all around us; it meant that the tidal stream had hold of us. It explained the breeze. It was a 'tide-wind'.

I reached for my hand-bearing compass to take another set of bearings. But Ushant had vanished, and so had Ile Vierge and the coastal crags. There was a beacon tower off the port bow, and it was drawing rapidly closer. It was also becoming fuzzy! The Ushant region is infamous for combined wind and fog.

The Fromveur Channel lay open but invisible, like the neck of a funnel into which that huge and monstrous flow of water poured, taking us with it. I felt panic. The little breeze was stronger now, waves were forming, there was a 'true' wind. We were closehauled on port tack. How long dared I stand on?

The helmsman looked at me. 'Keep her going,' I told him. The fog swirled and eddied between jib and staysail; the topsail was indistinct. Ahead was *nothing*. 'I want everybody on lookout. For *anything!*' I took over the helm.

I glanced over the side, judging speed – about four knots. So, half a mile in seven minutes. I dared not make more than half-mile tacks; the current was setting us to windward at maybe four knots. Navigation was impossible.

We were at the centre of a circle of swirling vapour. Around us the sea hissed and rustled like brown paper, the surface puckered and evil. A line of standing waves came at us and banged and boomed across our bow, spray splattering aft. A racing pigeon landed clumsily on our taffrail, dishevelled and lost. Lost, and yet it had to choose *us!* I knew its problem. It was the sort of bird that would queue at the wrong post office counter and claim its free gift the day after the offer closed. It crapped hugely on a coiled warp.

We stared into nothing, eyes aching. Somebody started chattering. 'Shut up and *concentrate!*'

The minutes passed. I tacked her. I kept her sailing full to have plenty of way on her in case it was needed in a hurry. It would be. Five minutes. More standing waves.

'There. Look!'

There was something low down and pale. Seconds later it was visible as a boil of water parting around rocks – an iron ladder – stonework rearing above.

I was heaving the wheel over, forcing myself not to slam it hard over and kill her headway. Our bowsprit arced round so slowly. 'God. Come ON!'

We seemed to hang in the wind with this great roaring wave

coming up on us, the tower looming over us. Then sails filled, the mass slid past our port quarter feet away and disappeared like a wraith. Something broke surface with water streaming from it and was gone. We slid forward into cotton wool nothing. I was shaking. We tacked twice after that, seven-minute boards with ten frightened people staring bug-eyed and dry of mouth. Then suddenly, quite simply, we sailed right out of the fog into a sunny evening and a profusion of buoys and marks to guide us on towards an anchorage in Cameret. I sighed shudderingly.

The pigeon, perched on a mounting heap of guano, gave me a nod. It had its feathers on inside out and looked thoroughly pissed off.

'We might try him with a little drop of bread and milk,' somebody said.

'We might try me with a snort of scotch. Hang on to this!' I said, quitting the wheel.

We went ashore in Cameret and dined a bit frugally but authentically at a fisherman's bistro. Crêpes, like asbestos lagging, washed down (a fair description) by an 'honest red'. The regulars eyed us silently and smoked hand-rollers that stank like an accident at Porton Down.

We carried the morning flood up the Gulet de Brest.

My reasons for going to Brest were that we could anchor within a short pull of the city and people could buy their shell-encrusted egg-timers – to give to 'them next door' for keeping an eye on the cat.

Then I spotted a quay with a yacht lying alongside. I hoped, forlornly, that nobody else had spotted it.

'Look, look, we could go in there!' some clown said, pointing. It was my ultimate engineless test. I resisted the temptation to take sail off, told the guardian angel to look the other way, and luffed for it.

We seemed to accelerate. I'll swear the wind increased. The luff went on and on. I adopted my foot-on-the-wheel pose, nonchalant, smile sagging, eyes popping. We were *going in too fast!*

People on the quayside took a few steps back. Our bowsprit pointed at them like Lord Kitchener's finger ... Your country needs you. What I needed was a miracle. We dropped alongside pretty as you like.

The other yacht was a sizeable ketch. There was one hell of a row going on, and a man loaded with kitbags was disembarking with another aboard the ketch yelling and pointing in a 'begone' sort of way. We learned that he was being dismissed for being a pain-in-the-butt. There was a French TV crew, and the skipper was a Scot. He told us that they were 'awa round the worrrld collecting the folklore of island and coastal folk. Fra' Pacific ter Antipodes, wi diving and ay!'

We lay alongside for a couple of days. The skipper of the ketch took me aside.

'You know yer seamanship, laddie,' he told me (knowing no better).

'We're a man short. We leave at dawn, and ye're welcome ter sign on!'

I couldn't though, could I. *Could I?*

How could I? I watched them go, waved them off. My heart was aching.

When we left there was a soft little offshore breeze, and we did things with springs and slip-ropes. I headed for the little-used eastern entrance of the great harbour wall, intending to explore the Rade de Brest.

On the Day of Armageddon, when the skies turn black, ripped and rent by lightning, when the earth explodes with volcanic eruption and earthquake, when tidal waves lay waste and the graves give up their dead, every harbour wall will still have its row of French anglers, berets set square, soggy dog-end stuck to lower lip, watching yachtsmen with baleful eye.

They lined the eastern entrance, scowling evilly, their lines athwart our way.

'Bon sewer mon sewers,' I hailed fluently, congratulating them on their drainage system, edging carefully around their lines. The bastards let us get well past then all started hollering together and in high good spirits. 'What are they on about?' I asked generally.

'We can't get out this way. The RAF bombed something. It's blocked!' an erudite bobble-hat explained.

I gybed all-standing, which was the quickest way to turn 180 degrees. Deep down I glimpsed masonry, kelp. Bang-bang, sheet home, scalp on end and soles of boots tingling in anticipation of the bump. The anglers reeled in, spat, cast again, and we were through and safe, heading back into the main harbour where the wind failed. We anchored. It was not turning out to be a good day for yachting.

The main harbour entrance lay about half a mile from us and across and beyond it the surface of the water was of that deep ultramarine shade which means that a breeze is blowing. Between it and us there was the glassiness of total calm.

We carried two ten-foot pulling dinghies, no outboards of course. I shrank from attempting a two-boat tow, having seen the wind-milling and weaving that went on when people rowed ashore. There was another option, but one I had never tried – the 'umbrella' warping technique which only needed two good rowers.

Here's how it works. You bend together every fathom of line you can find and attach a kedge to each end. One dinghy lays one anchor out ahead, and, as the crew haul her up to it, the *second* dinghy is taking the second anchor out. You 'walk' her along. It is possible to work up to a couple of knots, cover the deck with harbour filth, achieve total exhaustion, and do your back in – all of which we managed by the time we reached the entrance where our topsail filled and we laid closehauled on port tack. We headed for home, negotiating the Chenel du Four without bother.

We sailed back across-Channel in light airs making a landfall off Plymouth. I laid an inshore course across Bigbury Bay to stay within soundings in case we lost the wind and had to kedge. Which we did, off the Wembury firing range.

Up came a small naval launch in the charge of a rosy-cheeked midshipman, wearing a big cap.

'I say, you can't anchor here, there's a shoot on. You'll have to move!' he trilled. I explained the facts of life.

'Can't help that; you can't stay here!' this prat said.

'Then you'll just have to tow us.'

It seemed he wasn't 'empowered' to do anything so drastic as that. I told him it was tough tit, mate, so off he went to ask nanny what to do.

An hour later, having got clearance from Admiralty House, HM Queen and His Holiness the Pope, he was back, just as the wind filled in and we got under way.

We were bound back to Brixham where the engine was due to be fixed, and we carried both the breeze and the flood around Bolt and Start Point into Start Bay where both left us and the HM Customs cutter found us.

I always feel guilty in the presence of police or customs, which means I tend to crack jokes – further proof of my obvious guilt. Unsmiling official faces stare accusingly. I only once ever smuggled anything. Knowing nothing about wine – beyond the burping bottles of mother's vile elderberry in the airing cupboard – I smuggled a bottle which bore a label picturing a virulent-looking fruit. It turned out to be grenadine and about as alcoholic as mother's milk.

The cutter slowed close abcam. There was another huge official cap beneath which jutted a chin shaved to a high-gloss finish.

'Last port of call?' the cap wanted to know. I told it Brest.

'Brest,' it repeated, with innuendo, making it sound the last word in depravity. I should have said Sodom via Gomorrah.

'Stand by. I'm coming aboard skipper!' the Customs man said, doing just that.

I had always got on well with our home port Customs bloke, ever since he confiscated a miniature cactus garden from a woman who'd bought it in France. It was stubbled like a night-watchman's chin and probably carnivorous. It remained in quarantine on his parlour window sill being dosed with BabyBio.

But this man was for real. He scrutinised all passports, eyeing their owners with deep suspicion; sorted over their purchases with contempt, sucking his teeth and wagging his head. Eventually he got up to leave.

'My examination officer will be conducting a full search,' he said. 'I'll ask you again, *have you anything to declare?*'

There was the sort of hush that goes with judges donning black caps.

A young man in a boiler suit came aboard. 'I'll pick you up in Brixham,' Big-Cap said, gunning his engine before I could explain anything. The boiler suit man was called Alan, and he had a torch and a mirror on a stick. He crawled, poked, tapped, peered and probed everything from cable locker to butter dish. He had the lamps out of the sidelights, sails out of bags, and rockets out of box. He sniffed the vinegar bottle, measured the fuel tanks, looked wistfully at the toilet rolls, and settled for rattling the Harpic.

'Right then, skipper,' he said at last. 'Thanks for your cooperation.'

'No problem. How about a spot of tea?' I said.

He looked at his watch. 'Great,' he said.

The sails and spars were crashing about, but we weren't going anywhere.

'Er, when do you reckon we'll be in Brixham?'

'Good question,' I said. Then I explained.

It took another twenty-four hours to reach Brixham, the last couple of miles with a boat lashed either side, two oars in each. Alan loved every minute of it: the night watch-keeping, the sail trimming, kedging ... even the rowing.

The ICC borrowed boats. If the owner of a big yacht wanted to put her on ice for a bit, we took her over, fitted her out, maintained her to a high standard, insured her and used her, which was a damn sight better than leaving her swinging round a mooring covered with gull crap. There was a nice little ketch, *Nicolette*, down in Penryn, Cornwall. Joyce and I, plus another couple, went down there to fit her out. She was in a mess, having been unused for three or four seasons. We got the engine going and checked over sails, rigging and spars – wherein lies the rub.

Her varnish brightwork was hanging in ribbons. I took a swipe with a scraper, and then another. It was like picking a scab, I couldn't let it alone. Meanwhile my examination aloft was postponed, and when I finally got up there it was, if not perfunctory, less thorough than it should have been.

Mast-fittings and bands on wooden masts are potential trouble. My bradawl, inserted in the darkened area of wood where port spreader joined mast, went in easily and, worse than that, *came out easily*. A bradawl that can be pulled out with no resistance is bad news, but I decided, fatally, that 'with care' it should see us back to Salcombe. The wind was stuck in the sou'west on the starboard quarter for the passage east, so that was alright. Like curing a limp by walking with one foot in the gutter.

We motor-sailed from Falmouth with a faint southerly. It was warm and sticky; thunder rumbled. We hadn't been clear of St Anthony Head more than half an hour when it was on us. A thunderhead built up and boiled over like some monstrous duff. The rain hammered the sea into flat submission and then came the squall.

The whole thing became an absurdity: one moment we were sailing along in good order, then suddenly it was Widow Twankey time, revolving bow ties and a great deal of custard. The wind was supposed to be on our starboard quarter. It came at us from the opposite side; there came a crack from aloft as the spreader broke, followed at once by a louder one as the mast snapped at the hounds and the whole tangle of rope and sail descended upon us. Just to gift wrap the whole sorry mess our prop gobbled ten fathoms of slack halyard and we brought up solid.

I was luckier than I deserved. The lifeboat was at sea on exercise that very day.

Nicolette, skippered by Bill Purser, proved a popular club cruiser. Some years later she was to be sunk with tragic loss of lives in a horrifying manner.

She was cruising along quietly off the west Brittany coast when a fishing boat manned by drunks deliberately rammed and, despite Bill's frantic evasive twists and turns, sank her. The frightful matter occupied French law courts for years.

Quite by chance I heard a strange story that may shed some light on this maniacal and murderous behaviour. During the war the occupying German forces allowed the local fishing fleet, guardboat in attendance, to fish the coastal waters. It proved to be a perfect way for our agents to come and go, sneaking in by night while the guardboat was distracted. The local fishermen took fearsome risks.

Such was the tight security within our armed forces that this secret 'door' was known to few. The RAF air strike on the 'collaborating' fishermen was sudden and mortally effective.

Thereafter, in that locality, there grew up a hatred of the British which persisted. Drunken men, a British yacht, perhaps in the very waters where fathers, uncles had been gunned down?

The stranger entering Salcombe for the first time, noting the mighty bulk of Bolt Head to port and the wooded hills flanking the harbour on both sides, might be forgiven for anticipating peace and total shelter. The condemned man lays his neck upon the block; 'just a short back and sides, please,' he lisps.

The hard truth is that the wind funnels mightily down the valleys, and, when it is against a spring ebb, yachts at anchor sheer around, crossing their cables like some nightmare maypole dance, lacking only Morris dancers banging sticks. Nor is that all. Down at the entrance where the bar heaves and thunders, you can get a fair old swell running in, which, although within the mouth of the harbour, can break heavily in nearby Mill Bay.

Richard knew nothing of this when he sailed in one day in his newly bought Falmouth Quay Punt. Like others, he had sailed with the club and acquired a taste for sailing which led him to buy a boat of his own. He didn't know much about it. He didn't know, for instance, that a plunging barometer, mare's tails and a wind that backs agin the sun (trust it not for back 'twill run) were all excellent reasons for beginners to get the hell into shelter and stay there.

Up and down the harbour he sailed, showing off something rotten. Quay punts were designed to service square riggers at anchor in the roadstead – short masts to fit under the projecting yards of vessels when alongside and deep draught to cope with rough seas. Richard, in fact, had five foot six inches of water under him and a six-foot keel. The jolt shot his trousers down round his knees. She dried out; he walked ashore and came to me for help and advice. The tides were cutting, and he'd gone on shortly after high tide – gloomy factors demanding drastic measures.

'Get a bloke with a powerful boat,' I prescribed. 'By the next tide tonight it may well be blowing a hoolie!' High tide would be around 11pm. Meanwhile we laid out a stern kedge towards deep water.

Richard, his girlfriend Helen and I walked out and got aboard just as the water was starting to swirl around the rudder. The Punt, as you'd expect, was lying as flat as a motorway hedgehog, and, with a wait in prospect, we clambered below and shut the little companionway doors for it was blowing a bit by then ... not a notable gale but a vicious little low.

Once she was upright she began to slam and pound. We started the engine and put it full astern, clapped on to the kedge warp and tried to haul her out into deeper water. It was dark by then; it began to drag. The waves were now cresting and breaking against our transom with an abundance of spray. The bloke in the powerful boat turned up, took in the discouraging scene, waved dismissively and turned tail. Nobody thought about calling the lifeboat – not *inside the harbour*!

High tide time came and went. We retired below and had a go at Richard's gin, trying to ignore the spine-rattling crashes of keel on sand. We couldn't get ashore so we had no option. We sat there supping dismally, handing the bottle to and fro. Then came this deep rumble and a 'boom' as the wave hit our transom. A roaring of water

followed, and the little doors burst inward before the torrent. We sat up to our waists clutching glasses of gin and salt water.

'We must abandon ship!' I said unoriginally.

By God it was powerful stuff. Out in the cockpit Richard and I regarded one another. Faces streaming salt water, tight-lipped, jaws squared, our features working convulsively. Nobody spoke. With tight lips, squared jaws and features working convulsively, speaking isn't easy. Overhead a half-moon darted through ragged scraps of cloud like a plumber in the loft. Breaking waves boomed and surged; the water between us and the shoreline was completely white. Plainly we needed a lifeline, which meant a brave volunteer.

Richard insisted. Who was I to deny him? He was the owner; I was only there in an advisory capacity. The cockpit locker yielded masses of old halyard which he quickly knotted into a long, long line, the end of which he tied around his waist; without ceremony he hurled himself overboard and was gone. Cloud covered the moon, hiding him from view. I paid out line. Then I saw him on the beach in a slant of moonlight, and he was jumping about and waving in a curious fashion. So were we. The pounding and banging had increased. Our kedge warp was holding us bows-on to the beach, and each wave struck and parted as it hit our transom, dividing with a roar of foam. I urged Helen forward on hands and knees. There were no guardrails or pulpits. We sat bouncing on our bums while I hitched the line around her waist.

I was quite a long time fumbling around. 'That'll do!' she bawled in my ear, either in approval of my knots or disapproval of my fumbling. I helped her overboard with a shove and saw her drawn kicking shorewards. Then it was my turn. I 'recommended my soul to God' as they say, implying some sort of special offer – buy one get one free – then, filling my lungs, waited for a gap between bumps, and my lithe young body cleaved the water like an arrow. I stood up. The bloody water was only knee-deep.

She had her bows shoved up a steep ridge. Above the ridge was just foam and fuss. I waded ashore as Richard had done, unseen by us. Helen had ploughed a furrow with her boobs and was not best pleased. By morning the boat was a total wreck, split open like a kipper, spread along half a mile of beach and rock.

By the time the Island Cruising Club was into its third season we were cruising solidly from Whitsun until the middle of September. They were usually two week cruises: Channel Isles, North Brittany and back via Cornwall. We'd get back on Friday, one lot would leave next morning, we'd clean ship, take on stores, and the new bunch would arrive late afternoon all round-eyed and slapping around in their new plimsolls. We'd heave a long sigh and begin the tour of the ship, starting with the marine toilet, its use and the limits of its appetite.

We were getting people back for their second and third visits, and I was learning one heck of a lot about humanity but nothing about marital relationships.

I am now a *great*-grandfather with four grandchildren and a daughter conceived (I am certain) between the stopped-up storm trysail and the schooner fisherman staysail, in that sail locker. *Hoshi* being our only home it could hardly have been otherwise.

Our marital relationship needed a jolt, and this was it. What now? We had fifty pounds in the bank, our belongings stowed in tin rocket-boxes and no prospects whatsoever. I had continued to write, which was like playing pelota against editorial ramparts. Editors' rejection slips mounted. They thanked me for showing them my work – implying a hasty peep at something nasty in a matchbox – but regretted (a damn sight less than I did) that they were unable to use it. None of the rejection slips were tear-stained.

When it came, the jolt had thirteen thousand tons of ship behind it, and Joyce was about four months gone, asleep in the sail locker and clutching her cat.

We were approaching the end of a cruise, reaching over a smooth sea and some twelve miles from Salcombe. It was eleven o'clock at night. To our east, to windward and maybe three miles away, a large ship was heading in towards Prawle Point and the Lloyd's signal station, a common enough practice. It meant that we were on roughly parallel courses, no cause for alarm and no need for action on our part.

In the early fifties yachts didn't carry radar reflectors. Our navigation lights were twelve volt, and we were showing only one small green to the ship. Routinely I shone the powerful duty torch towards her and then panned it over our sails. We rolled along at our comfortable four knots, chatting quietly around the wheel.

Then the ship, now well inshore, altered on to a more westerly heading, shaping now to cross our bows as she headed for open waters, as might be expected. Then, all at once, she altered further and further to port until she was heading straight offshore and on a parallel course to us, maybe a quarter of a mile to the east.

I sat up and took notice, and got busy with the torch again. She was safe enough so long as she held that course, passing clear up our starboard side, but I never took my eye off her and thank God I didn't. She was a black, light-studded mass against the stars, and I could hear her tonk, tonk, tonking engine, a metallic heartbeat. Then she turned on us.

The shape narrowed until it was a black axe, heaving higher as it came, bow-wave bellowing, rearing higher and higher. I was spinning the wheel and yelling something, bearing away from her, reducing the target, and my eyes never left that awful sight.

The wheel was hard down, but our bows seemed to bear off with dream-like slowness. I felt a sort of lethargy, almost peace, numbed I suppose. Joyce was now clutching her cat beside me. The monstrous thing came ripping down our starboard side, gear rained from aloft, wet, black steel plates with rows of rivets, our guardrail curling back and a dinghy scrunching, water swept our deck.

Then she was past. She stopped half a mile away. We were in chaos with people struggling to get on deck, me struggling to get below to assess damage. Were we sinking? A woman, a chain-smoker, fought her way past me, returning for her fags. 'We're going to die!' a man gabbled.

We were not sinking.

I started the engine and motored over to the ship. Nobody wanted to give me her name, then the Captain, stripey in pyjamas, cried out '*Beaver*! *Beaver Lodge*.'

With our rig hanging like a broken wing we motored home. Twice there came coasters, alerted by *Beaver Lodge* to look out for us, shining searchlights, signalling. I could only wave them off. For Christ's sake don't *come near*!

We were not badly damaged apart from the deck being sprung by the concussion, and the damages were sorted between the insurance companies. I only heard what had happened on the grapevine.

It seemed that a young fourth mate had panicked. In standing to the westward he came on a collision heading with a distant inward-bound ship, so he altered ninety degrees offshore – only to discover a second collision situation with an *outward* bound ship. Nobody even saw us.

It was pretty obvious that we needed a home – a retreat ashore. There was a derelict, condemned cottage. I bought five quid's worth of spring-twanging furniture in the auction rooms, and, with the owner's connivance, I squatted.

It was one of a row of two-roomers built into the hillside. Inside forty-eight hours, aided by a team from the club, we gutted, painted, glazed and papered it, adding chintzy curtains, a bowl of flowers and a brass door-knocker. The crash-squad of housing officers and health officials, with brown boots and waistcoats, could find no fault. The cottages had outdoor loos. *You never spotted women neighbours actually entering or leaving them.* The old couple next door lived in squalor and their cottage had to be fumigated. Their fleas emigrated via the stone party wall and invaded us, costing us a bomb in Keatings. When you relaxed into an armchair there was a whoosh, and you vanished in a white cloud like a pantomime fairy. Visitors took in the roses round the door. 'Aren't you lucky!' they'd say.

The following year (1955) came an offer from Bill Smart, editor of *Yachts and Yachting*; there was a job on the magazine's editorial staff if I wanted it.

I was a father. I couldn't afford *not* to want it.

My first editorial cock-up • Blood spouted •
Keith and the Romano-Brits
• A spinnaker run

Southend-on-Sea in Essex, where *Yachts and Yachting* had (and still has) its office, is a red-brick tide stretching from Leigh, via Westcliff and Southend, to Shoebury in the east. It is an unbroken sprawl of pebble-dash, bay and impenetrable lace curtain, a roost for London-bound commuters who daily disappeared 'up the line' in their charcoal grey and pinstripe. One day I was to join this dawn flight.

Meanwhile, from my desk, I could admire my view. By leaning forward and craning my neck I could see a rectangle of sky above a brick cliff upon which massive sanitation drains curved and writhed, as though the building had been disembowelled. It was a far, far cry from the soaring cliffs of Devon, and my heart mourned.

I had never worked in an office. I was a caged bird. It would take more than a little mirror and a sprig of millet to comfort me. In my first week, to make it noteworthy, I wrote an article containing a major error.

I correctly quoted a 'cable's length' as being roughly two hundred yards, and, being cautious, to check this out I picked the only reference book in the office that contained an error.

A cable, it lied, was roughly four hundred yards. I heaved a sigh of relief and re-wrote the article. It was published.

The readers skinned me alive. 'Such an error could cost lives!' they fluted happily. Bill read their letters. 'Ho, ho, ho, ho,' he rumbled grinning.

We published a letter, allegedly from me, which ran 'A cable-is-a-cable-is-a-cable' for two inches of column. It was signed Des Sleightholme's homework.

Bill was a Falstaffian figure: mighty of belly, eyebrows like a thatched porch, and a deep bass of a voice. In his time he had been a cavalryman, gunboat skipper, racing car driver, trawlerman under sail, boys' story writer, secret agent and editor.

He had been in the Balkans on the eve of World War II, charged with planting demolition charges on German river barges. These arrived from the Naval dockyard, Pompey, crated and labelled 'High explosives, use no hooks', broad arrows everywhere.

Bill had a caustic wit. To a big-head author whose copy was both overdue and overrated he remarked frowningly, 'So the lion has at long last given birth to a mouse!'

With wartime chums he launched *Yachts and Yachting* in a back bedroom. Ex-offshore yachtsman and founder-member of the Royal Ocean Racing Club, Bill's stomach ulcers ended his sailing; now he had me as his proxy.

I went on the RORC crew list or 'pierhead-jumpers benefit'. Racing owners occasionally found themselves a hand short. Accordingly you got to sail on all manner of boats varying from spearhead fliers to Class three walking wounded, all excellent experience and a guarantee of suffering. I could have time off to go racing provided it was not what Bill called a 'lady's race', which meant that it ended up somewhere nice.

My first ever race was the Harwich to Hook, which, while it ended up nicely enough in the Hook of Holland, practically guaranteed privation, penance and a satisfactory helping of pain.

Biddy Smart, the Yachts and Yachting *editor's wife. We shared an office and a similar sense of humour. Her dog bedded under my desk and farted non-stop. She denied it vehemently. There was no justice.*

It started gently on a run that, by nightfall, had become a gallop terminating with a lightship around which yachts converged out of the blackness. There were yells and curses, slamming gybes and ringing sheet winches.

The light beam swept round and round illuminating little vignettes of suffering, like some church hall tableau, rich in moral inspiration.

It illuminated the cock-up as we got our spinnaker down and genny up. Somebody smacked me over my dome with a winch handle; blood spouted. I tottered back to the cockpit, which was now knee-deep in rope and filled with struggling crew. The owner noted my condition with deep compassion.

'Aw fer Gawd's SAKE!' he bellyached, 'Don't go bleedin' all over the place. Somebody'll slip and hurt themselves!'

One crew member was a Harley Street surgeon. He whipped out his yachting knife, slashed off a lock of my hair and smacked a sticky on the gash.

We came hard on the beat for Smith's Knoll, ninety miles to the north. The bloody boat stood on her tail, wham-bang-crash. 'God!' I groaned *ninety miles of this!*

'I know, I know,' mourned a racing freak. 'We could do with double, but there you are!'

Joyce got her old job back as editor's PA while my mother looked after baby daughter Michele. It was the only way we could save a bit of money. My twelve quid a week was princely after the ICC pay of four quid and all the pilchards I could scoff.

Bill and Biddy Smart lived in an old Coastguard cottage in Leigh where, long ago, Mister A had munched and smiled his smile. In time, we raised the down payment on the cottage next door. Leigh-on-Sea suited us. It was a muddy place, and I'd graduated in mud.

Old Leigh survived as a lost fragment of nineteenth century England separated from suburbia by the railway tracks, hanging by its fingertips, and facing the wide saltings of the Thames Estuary. There were ramshackle cockle, whelk and shrimp stalls surrounded by heaps of shells, lapped by each tide.

Old men in pubs could still be heard to say 'werry' instead of 'very', as they did in the reigns of the Georges. Their past as smugglers and wreck plunderers was still part of ordinary conversation. Said old man Turnnidge of his father and the uncomfortable matter of a ransacked schooner aground on the Buxey, 'Twas a danged lie I tell you; she weren't a schooner – she wuz a ketch!'

We bought a little 22-ft gaff cutter in Wivenhoe. She had been laid up against a wall – her east-facing side was so dry you could shake hands through her seams. Her engine had been in a junk Morris, marinized by a maniac. You put the gear lever ahead to go astern. The throttle consisted of a threaded rod and a nut; if you needed to throttle back in a hurry you had to roll up your sleeve like a vet at the birth of a calf and swipe your bare arm over it. When (if) it was started from cold you opened a water bleeder cock and copped a jet of hot rust.

Cygnet. *You could post letters through her topside planking when we bought her. Her engine had been taken out of an old Morris car, in haste.*

Office routine meant proof-reading and hammering out banal club news. I edited a page called A to Z, an alphabet of weirdo words such as 'malgogger' and 'snottle-dog'; readers won a guinea for sending them in, which meant that the bastards got inventive. 'Waauff', offered one, 'a square Indian canoe, named from the cry of the user when attempting to paddle it.'

Bill's maxim was to never let the reader flip through an issue unmoved. He may be instructed, entertained, amused or bloody furious, but he must never, never remain indifferent. So, among other titillations, we published nautical pin-ups with huge boobs encased in red/green port and starboard bras.

Furious readers wrote in. Said one, 'Sir, I am a clean-minded young naval officer ...' Bill wrote a reply by return.

'Sir, there is no such thing as a clean-minded young naval officer!'

There was a Southsea-to-Harwich race when we lost our mast in the Dover Straits and another miserable Harwich to Copenhagen event when our forestay pulled the stem hook apart as though dismembering a chicken. Yachts were still wood built; overtightening shrouds could open up a garboard strake like lifting yourself up by your boot tabs. Some Class Three leaders pumped their way around the courses.

Bill would follow the races in simulation from chart, tidal atlas, pilot and shipping forecast. If I was late back I stood to get a bollocking. 'You had a fair stream and an easterly force six. What kept you?'

I had a sailing mate, Keith, a laconic aircraft engineer who kept the engine running – if the shattering bangs and grinding of a straight-through gearbox rated the description. Winter weekends we spent up the Medway exploring the creek beds at low tide. We found things. Sometimes gruesome things, for this particular creek was once the quarantine or 'plague' anchorage, where London-bound ships from messy climates lay until deemed clean enough to proceed up-river. Here also lay the prison hulks. The numerous dead from both sources were simply dumped for the crabs to sort out.

In The Crooked Billet pub in Leigh one day, medical students were bemoaning the price of skeletons for study – it was long before fibreglass copies. 'Skillingtons?' interrupted an old wildfowler, alert to the chance of profit. 'You wants a skillington? I can find plenty o' them, mate. Fiver a time all right?'

It was a December afternoon, low spring tide, grey, spitting with sleet as we trudged the creek bed. It was a very low tide and mud was exposed that we'd never seen before. We'd found old pop bottles, baccy pipes and a thought-provoking profusion of brass fly buttons – a rich archaeological treasure – and now there was broken pottery. It was black with a rudimentary pattern: shards of jars, bowls. We filled our bucket then moved on.

It was getting dusk, and the flood was making. It was time to get back to the dinghy. We turned and headed for it. I was leading, Keith following. I heard him curse and looked round. He was on the new patch, up over his boots. Very funny. I laughed heartily. He tried to take a step and went down flat, and then, suddenly, it wasn't funny anymore. His arms were in up to the shoulder, and his face was blank, scared. I couldn't reach him.

'Hang on, I'll go get the oars!' I said, stupidly, since he couldn't move. I tried to run, but it was like running in glue. By the time I got back I was knackered. It was nearly dark now; Keith was barely controlling panic. The advancing tideline was yards away.

I shoved the oars under his armpits and we struggled. It was a nightmare. I was beginning to sink as well. Then quite suddenly he

Leigh Creek, the 'third world' of yachting and my particular delight. Winkles and wellies, a squelching ambience of motor tyre fender and rowlocks round your neck.

Start of a Fastnet race in Galloper *(photographer unknown). We were to lose a man overboard, recovering him with difficulty and learning one hell of a lot in the process.*

was free. We got him out minus his boots. We didn't say a word.

Back on board, with Keith in his sleeping bag and a double scotch in Keith, he said something very odd. He said. 'It wasn't so much like sinking. It was as if *something was dragging me down by my feet!*'

Later I took some of our pottery to the museum. The curator was positive about it. 'Grave goods, Romano-British, probably fourth century. An old burial ground!' he stated. I gulped. Something dragging me down?

The up-creek yachtsman, trudging high booted over flooded saltings, rowlocks dangling around his neck, crabs scuttling, is dear to my heart – this is the 'third world'of yachting, far removed from the deck shoe and designer labelled down-river yachtie of the marina fringe.

I had a boot in both worlds. Racing, I would crank sheet-winches worth more than my entire boat, join in urging an owner to buy 'us' a new genny, chuck out a spinnaker. But that was what owners were for – chequebooks on legs.

I pier-head jumped aboard boats where the weight and rotundity of your seabag stigmatised you like a hint of contagious disease. I learned to carry it hooked over a finger with airy indifference when boarding, despite gritted teeth and a twitching jaw muscle. 'Weight' was all. An extra pair of socks was regarded as hedonism. Everybody spoke in terse monosyllables, and the helmsman never spoke at all. Nor was he spoken to.

On one occasion somebody gave the helmsman a biscuit at tea-up time. The owner went spare.

'Biscuits! Don't feed the helmsman biscuits!' he thundered as if conducting children round a zoo. *'I couldn't race and eat biscuits!'* The helmsman sat there, crumbs falling from lifeless lips.

Other boats might be crack racing machines from half an hour before a race until ten seconds after the start, when it became patently clear to all that the owner had loused up the start. 'At least we've got our wind clear!' he would protest to deaf ears and the birds. The redeeming feature was that, if you were a lousy racing yachtsman, at least there was always somebody worse. Every boat had its chummy-ship, and every race would break up into a dozen little unofficial duels.

There was a Fastnet race in which the ketch I was crewing had a ding-dong going with a fat little cutter of similar size and uselessness. All the way down-Channel we swapped tacks with her, then lost her west of the Scillies. We rounded the Rock alone and in a drizzle. The lighthouse keeper, driven wild by the stirring sight, raised one finger in salutation. It was a soggy run until we had Bishop Rock astern, and then the wind stiffened and we handed our spinnaker in a six rising seven. Then, from astern, out of the gloom, came our rival still under spinnaker and going like the Edinburgh express. Our owner went passionate.

'Up, up, get our spinny up quick, quick!' he howled, dancing up and down. We did so, albeit with misgivings. Black night and a rising wind, yacht yawing and boring into the blackness with the helmsman pop-eyed with funk and fighting the broach. Hour after hour we ran neck-and-neck, our rival's port light swerving as she yawed, spinnaker monstrous against the stars.

We lost our spinnaker in a welter of rag and bloody knuckles and fell astern. Our owner sulked all the way to Plymouth and the finishing line. Later, we met the other crowd. Our owner started going on about how he'd never have packed it in if our sail hadn't blown.

'Daft bugger!' the other skipper said. 'Ours was stuck. We couldn't get it down!'

Top table • Snappy and the foam • Who stole the police boat?

I became an after dinner speaker. Yacht clubs invite magazines to produce guest speakers,

'Here you are', said Bill. 'Time you did one of these ...' as if it was some sort of wire puzzle. I bought a used dinner jacket and pants altered by a tailor whose client had either died or defaulted. They made me feel debonair, rake-helly, a bit of a lad. My daughter, then age seven, said devastatingly, 'Daddy looks like Charlie Chaplin.'

After dinner speaking and proposing toasts is dangerous. 'I'd like to propose a test to our ghosts,' mumbled one petrified tyro. The first lesson

Daughter Michele. 'Daddy looks like Charlie Chaplin!' she laughed healthily when I appeared in my first dinner jacket.

is go easy on the pre-dinner drinks and don't let them top up your wine. At top table I sat by the Commodore's wife who was a bit deaf. She asked what I sailed and did I race. I said I'd only got a small boat. 'What?' she said.

'I've only got a little one,' I howled, for the benefit of the first four tables. Some wag said 'hear, hear'.

I was in fine form though, face glowing, knocking things over, a born raconteur at table. Then it was my turn.

I rapped out my pipe into the All-comers Points Crystal Salver, due to be presented later, and rose unsteadily.

Bonhomie drained out of me like a punctured sump. I stood swaying, deaths-head rictus of a grin fading ... It was quite dreadful. I forgot my stories (or mixed them), I deleted the punch-lines and yet the audience rocked with mirth, tears streaming. 'Easy,' I thought, not realising that my clip-on dicky bow tie was hanging by one claw like a bat and due to fall off into my brandy.

My next attempt was even worse. 'Try a tranquillizer,' somebody advised and gave me one. It was huge; all it lacked was a warhead and fins. Plainly it must not be taken too soon or left too late; midway between the last courses seemed right.

My plan was to palm it into my mouth under cover of a cough, which means forming a funnel with the hand. The funnel acted like the deadly poison dart blowpipe of the primitive jungle hunter.

The pill shot forth with force and accuracy, bounding away between the diners sitting opposite, its flight followed by all eyes as it disappeared under the next table. A hunt ensued. 'There, there!' cried sportsmen. A waiter retrieved it and returned it to me reverently on a platter with a glass of goddam water.

All eyes were upon me as I sipped and swallowed. What fearsome and terminal illness did it portend? They listened in compassionate silence to my address and laughed too loudly at my funny stories. Their eyes seemed to be saying 'his jokes may be crap but by God he's brave!'

I invented a character called 'Old Harry', a combination of Derek from the past and 'Snappy' Noakes of the present. Snappy was a navy blue figure, cloth capped like a stoppered bottle, bulbous of nose and with a doorstep lower lip – one of those people about whom legends abound.

He was the Leigh Creek 'huffler' or mud-pilot. He ran a shilling sicker off Southend beach, and he sold boats to anybody innocent enough, sufficiently besotted and stupid enough to buy one. His sales pitch was typical.

'Do she 'andle easy?' he'd ask rhetorically. 'Why I can stand on the shore, mate, and whistle 'er in like a dawg!'

He had a wife 'up the line', a local euphemism meaning she'd left him and gone back home up Dagenham way. You could identify his waterfront cottage by the grey vests and woollen Union suit combinations pegged out like the pelts of some trapper.

Snappy was the permanent nightmare of the Foreshore Parks and Gardens Department that regularly summoned him to appear before it. A favourite story told how he once up-ended the trestle table, resulting in a fine show of sock suspender and pink bloomer.

His boat was always overloaded with trippers. 'Why they must'a snook aboard quiet', he would explain, hinting at their desperation to patronise his, rather than a rival's, boat.

Certainly his trips were different, his spiel being concerned not with such educational topics as the length of the pier but with death and mutilation.

'She wuz run dahn abaht *'ere'*, he would say of a now defunct rival sicker-boat. 'Blood and hentrails everywhere!' Or he might describe corpses he'd come across. 'Abaht 'ere I see'd it. Crabs a'swimmin aht its mouf mate!' Passengers would peer around, alert for floating cadavers. He came to me, a man of letters, in the hope that I would publish his woes and bring justice to bear.

He had a disturbing trick of grasping his listeners by their coat lapels and rocking them to and fro by way of emphasis. It seemed that he had had the Board of Trade inspector sicked on him by the FPG Dep. He must attend to his safety equipment at once or suffer loss of licence. He borrowed the necessary equipment from his mates but the BOT inspector, finding the fire extinguisher to be empty, held up the hand of authority: no licence until the matter was rectified. Snappy gave him a lot of lip.

He barrowed the empty appliance up Leigh hill to the fire station where a mate filled it with foam for free. The BOT man came back. 'Ah, but do it work, skipper, do it work?' that cunning official demanded evilly. 'Why ercourse it works!' Snappy scorned, pressing the tit. It worked relentlessly and unstoppably.

With sorrow-racked features he told the story, rocking me with vigour. 'There I was a'swipin' and a'scoopin' wiv me cap, mate!' He released me, and, removing his cap, demonstrated both method and

Joyce, Thames Barge Sailing Club 1956. She has a eye on the weft and looks a bit uncertain.

accompanying footwork. 'All me bleedin' foam, mate, '*GORN!*'

Then there was another Old Harry ingredient in Bob Roberts, sailing barge-master and seaman. He was a short, broad man with a round face and a gappy grin such as a child might draw. He walked straddle-legged, dangling huge, battered hands. He was the sort of man who would have sailed with Drake in *Golden Hind*.

His sailing barge, *Cambria*, was the last engineless merchant vessel in the land. He traded the East Coast winter and summer, and I was lucky enough to make three or four passages in her. Lacking a car, joining her up some remote creek was difficult or I'd have sailed more often.

I learned much from Bob. Shooting a dock, for instance. Luff and shoot. Every occasion could be different depending on cargo weight. It was miraculous. I stood on the lock at West India dock one windy night as *Cambria* loomed up in the darkness, luffing, everything banging. An official watched in horror.

'Christ, he'll pile her up!' he gasped.

She shot the locks all a'shake; there was a becket on the wheel. Bob was peeing over the stern. 'That you, Des?' he bellowed jovially.

He navigated by hand-lead and looking at the water. The only chart was dated 1914, and it lined his cabin drawer. The binnacle compass, with a sack on it, was the dog's day-bed, and the navigational data was a brewer's calendar giving the times of high water. London Bridge. He had a rhyme:

'High tide London Bridge,
Low tide in the Swin,
Half-flood in Yarmouth Roads,
Half ebb at Lynne' – or something of the sort.

Where Bob went so did his melodeon and repertoire of barging songs, some of them a bit raw for delicate listeners. He favoured bargemen's pubs: those drab, square, Victorian relics shunned by tourists. Entering the Thames once, we ran out of fair tide and anchored. There was a pub. Bob was greeted with the usual bargeman's acclaim. 'How-do, Bob. Not drownded yet.'

It was a fine evening of smoke and beer, sweating, hollering men and stamping boots. We left after midnight, Bob reeling from the free drinks which were his perk. It was a bright moonlit night with a hard, hard frost, and some bastard had stolen our boat.

'Them Dutchies getting back aboard!' Bob reckoned, referring to some Dutch sailors who'd left the pub earlier. There was another pulling boat though. She was lying moored fore and aft, no sweeps in her, but who cared. We paddled her back to *Cambria* with the bottom boards, singing to the moon, me attempting close harmony with some success. We streamed her astern and turned in. Bob was very pissed.

It was a hail that woke me. I stuck my head out. A motor barge was going by. A man said, 'Tell Bob the police boat is hunting for its bleedin' tender, and you've got it lyin' astern. 'Ere she comes now!' he added, pointing.

I shook Bob awake. I nearly had to break his arm. He bleared his way on deck, took in the crisis and reacted instantly, smoothly and craftily. The police boatmen had spotted their boat. They were licking their chops, getting their notebooks out. 'You officers owe us a drink!' said Bob. 'Saved your boat for you!'

After working on *Yachts and Yachting* for twelve years I fell out with Bill and went freelance. I had taken on a column in the local paper. It was far removed from yachting and dealt with such diverse subjects as windmills, hot-air ballooning and Victorian plumbing in particular, the 'drains rocket' – a device implying rows of toilet users leaping to their feet with smouldering shirt-tails. Bill wanted body and soul.

I kept up my regular *Y and Y* stuff, plus short stories and anything that came along including being yachting correspondent for the *Sunday Observer*. I was not sorry to be out of the office with Biddy's dog farting under my desk then tiptoeing away and Bill, the omnipotent, looming over my life. Nonetheless Bill taught me my trade and sent me sailing – six Fastnets and a permanent soaking.

The *Observer* job meant pre-dawn Saturday morning starts to reach the sailing venue, bumping down lanes, the occasional badger grumbling its way home being the only traffic. I saw a lot of gravel pits and dinghies and buzzing powerboats.

The Round the Island race was a struggle. It began at Cowes and, to cover the major turning points, it meant driving like the wrath of God to The Needles where you watched the leaders go round. Then you waited to see the leaders of Class III and drove flat-assed to St Catherine's Point, saw the leaders, and so on.

Having sailed the race and watched a few, I soon learned to write most of my copy in advance and in various versions according to wind and weather. We all did that. One poor clot thought he'd cover the race from home, but he got his notes mixed. His copy read, 'rounded Bembridge under gossamer sails in the merest whisper ...' It was blowing seven rising eight.

The first Cowes/Torquay International Power Boat Race was another pain. I covered it in extreme discomfort from the after-deck of a very high-speed RAF tender, my coccyx driven up to my collar-stud, notepad reduced to dripping pap and my ballpoint about as much use as Hamlet's dagger. On arrival, with deadline pressing, I phoned in five hundred words of blatant Enid Blyton with hard facts as sparse currents in a workhouse: duff but colourful. Next morning I was on the train heading home. A yachtsman sat down opposite and started reading his *Sunday Observer*. My stuff was an edge of page single column. He read it. I wondered whether to make myself known, but my guardian angel said, 'No, don't be a prat!' Having read it carefully *he tore it out*!

I thought, 'My God, this is fame. Too good to throw away eh!' Then the bastard took off his cap, folded my deathless prose into a narrow strip and fitted it inside the sweatband. He replaced his cap.

'That's better!' he told me.

Freelance and a sort of PR • A special punch
• To be an editor

Freelancing means that the moment you stop working you stop earning. Consequently you are tempted to grab every job and opportunity that comes along. My *Y and Y* regular features paid the milkman, but it put no cherries on the cake. The America's Cup job offered a fat pay cheque.

Back in the days of the *Sceptre* challenge I had been given time off to crew on the trial horse 12 Metre, *Evaine* owned by Owen Aisher the Marley-tile millionaire. It was all very exciting, even if the ultimate performance of *Sceptre* against her American rival was like watching Morris dancers perform Swan Lake.

Now it was happening again, *Sovereign* versus the Aisher-Livingstone *Kurrewa V*, fighting for the chance to be hammered into the ground by the American defence. I was employed as a sort of PR to Owen Aisher.

The 12 Metre Evaine *and bum of professional skipper Stan Bishop, the only man I ever saw who was driven to biting then jumping on his own cap.*

It began at Gosport. One Friday afternoon Aisher said to me, 'You'd better get over there with a spy camera and see what they're up to!'

I had a clear two days to get a visa, get sorted and over there. First to Oyster Bay, Long Island. I arrived jet lagged on the last train of the day. It was midnight but I needed lodgings. There was a taxicab. I climbed aboard. The driver looked at me with deep suspicion. He asked, 'You carryin' bud?'

'Am I carrying what?'

'One of dese!' he said, lugging a six-shooter out of the glove compartment. He was more helpful about accommodation. He offered me a straight choice. 'Motel or whore-house?' He pronounced it 'ho'house'.

Being a nice boy who always ate up his greens, I didn't know what the hell he was talking about and said so.

'*Cat-house*, bud,' he translated. 'Or don't you limey guys do nuthin' but play cricket!'

Using Aisher's limitless funds I chartered a sixty-foot Chris-Craft cruiser, complete with skipper, and went hunting. Every day we headed out into Long Island Sound where the American defenders were exercising. We kept out of their way but within long lens range. I banged off roll after roll.

The yanks were on to me instantly. They struck poses. Chin on finger, hand on hip and one dropped his pants, all very secret. We cheered and waved to each other.

I flew home with my reels. I reported to the Royal Thames Yacht Club with a written report on every aspect of American defence including crew sex life, plus a fat stack of whole plate glossies. I expounded in person on the new twin pole gybing technique and the lightning magazine headsail change.

'Jolly good, jolly good!' said Important Members and did nothing. It wasn't really *yachting*, was it? One felt that twin pole gybes were faintly caddish, like cheating at golf.

I returned to the States later when *Sovereign* and *Kurrewa V* were shipped over. Crews were billeted in large mansions in Newport. My job was PR-cum-fix-it man. I had also to try to keep the *Kurrewa* gorillas off the nubile hired help (all good catholic girls) and act as Owen Aisher's social secretary. I was a cross between parish priest and Jeeves.

I'd show him the invitations as he breakfasted. If nobody special would be there I would refuse them. If he heard later that somebody important *would* be there, I'd have to eat crow, act the dumb limey and amend his refusal. He was paying.

Aisher made his millions by being an opportunist of vision. As a police cadet and home on leave he found that his dad, a jobbing builder, had come by a tile making machine that was 'bloody useless'. Owen built a fortune from it. His tiles hit the markets just as D.I.Y mania arrived. He never stopped work. Twice at receptions he called me over. 'See this flooring,' he mouthed sideways, while beaming around, 'Get a sample back to the factory *now!*' I would have to seek out the domestic staff and flash a few dollars. When the hula hoop craze hit America Aisher phoned the factory. 'Save all offcuts of 25mm tubing, weld them into 70cm (or whatever) circles, store them and wait!' A few weeks later he cleaned up the market.

The Cup Challenge was the usual rout. Aisher flew home before it was over. He was an uneasy boss. I took it upon myself to buy some small key fob souvenirs for the domestic staff and handed him the modest bill. 'You pay it!' he snapped. 'I never authorised it!'

I flew home a bit poorer but wiser.

I had written a book entitled, with numbing lack of originality, *Cruising.* It meant throwing a book launch party at which a special punch would be served. 'It will be *extra*-special!' I predicted with uncanny prescience. I took wine, brandy, a whole bottle of Cointreau and, fatally, an egg. I put pan on cooker. It doesn't take *cordon bleu* status to know what heat does to eggs.

'Well here's to the book', somebody toasted.

'Success to the book!' chorused my guests, raising their spoons in salute. They don't make custard like that anymore.

I wrote freelance for four years and then in 1966 an advert appeared in *The Times.* An editor was wanted for *Yachting Monthly.* Joyce said, 'You're applying and no nonsense!' Neither was there.

I was interviewed by Maurice Griffiths over lunch at The Ritz. He had been editor for forty years barring war service, which was distinguished – hairy, scary and earning him a George Medal for dismantling live enemy mines. He watched me narrowly but benignly, and then took me on between sweet and coffee.

MG was a legend. His brand of sailing was modest and hugely evocative. His books inspired hundreds of readers to emulate it. The

MG-way meant the Thames Estuary swatchways, that labyrinth of tidal guts and channels along the Essex and Suffolk coasts. It was a 'cabin lamp' cult. The little ship punching into the small, steep chop, bringing up for the night in some lonely creek where curlews call. Then came the yellow glow of a paraffin lamp and a sizzling frying pan, followed by pipe smoke and the swapping of yarns, then deep, sweet sleep lulled by the gentle slap of wavelets.

It was gentle, evocative stuff and within the reach of all dreamers. It no longer exists. Nowadays the dream is of coral lagoon and Cape Horn.

When the magazine was taken over by a big group MG lost interest; he told me so. He was a small dapper man with a pointed beard, Edwardian, very correct, a bit intimidating. On my first day I shared his office. The building was once the headquarters of the suffragettes. Gas fires bubbled; an ancient lift rumbled and clanked.

He called for his secretary. 'Take a letter, Miss Brown.'

She was petite, and she wore a mini-skirt like an economy lampshade. She crossed her knees. I studied the ceiling in desperation. When she'd finished the letter we watched her exit with the intensity of ornithologists studying a rarity. Which was how I discovered MG's hidden depths ... He let out a deep and shuddering sigh. 'That,' he said, 'is what I think they call a pussy-pelmet.'

I joined the magazine in 1966 and took over as editor six months later. Maurice Griffiths, Norman Clackson, the office and advertisement manager, and Kathy Palmer, assistant editor, all retired together, leaving me a team of three including Miss pussy-pelmet Brown. There were also two matrons in a back room doing accounts and subscriptions. 'Keep clear, they bite!' MG warned me.

I sidled in, bent upon a warm and democratic relationship.

'Hi,' I said, 'Everybody calls me Des!' One was bowed over her desk, the other was thumping a rubber stamp. She looked at me over her half-lenses. 'How unfortunate, *Mister* Sleightholme!' she said, thumping away.

Then a well-wisher took me aside. He thought I ought to know that the magazine was scheduled for closure in six months time unless it bucked up its circulation. I had to do something. I was free to do anything provided it didn't cost money. There was a racing section mainly written by dear old gentlemen who hadn't raced since the Kaiser was at Cowes Week, and it was never less than three months out of date. Between one issue and the next I chopped it. Nobody complained; *nobody* even noticed! One old man phoned up and mumbled something in a reedy voice.

I introduced humour and lots of stuff about how to execute a 'gravesend luff' and how to make things. Circulation began to pick up at once. There were pitfalls.

The boat test, the 'product review', is the banana skin which has been the wailing downfall of many an editor. You publish a glowing description of a product and the Ad Manager, on the strength of it, sells space. If it is a lousy product angry readers demand blood and you lose 'editorial integrity'. Like virginity, you don't lose it twice.

There were a lot of lousy boats being built as fibreglass began to take hold. We reviewed them with costly and truthful naivety. MG had built up magazine integrity. I wasn't going to lose it.

Most rivals prevaricated. It was like 'estate agent-ese'. 'Generous headroom' meant boxy: she sails like an allotment shed. 'This delightful little boat is within reach of every pocket', meant substandard plywood and crappy fittings. 'A powerful little boat that takes some holding,' meant vicious weather helm. An Advertisement Director 'had a little chat with me'.

Magazine readers elevate editors and inflate their egos as if plying a foot pump. Some become insufferable. I was in the lobby of the Cafe Royal waiting for Joyce to take her coat off. A senior editor waited with me. Fellow guests were flooding in, a tide of dicky-tie, corsage and agonising footwear. The senior editor bowed to some old bat in a vast nightie. He said to me, 'In the eyes of my readers I suppose I am a God-like figure. I don't know them, but *they all know me*.'

'Like the gents' toilet attendant', I suggested.

Maurice Griffiths never offered advice. 'If you want anything, ring me, otherwise I'll let you get on with it!'

It wasn't easy to wear his trousers. He'd been editor since most readers were infants; he had *always* been editor. When I introduced myself as the YM editor old men wobbled their chins at me.

'No you're not. The editor's a feller called – on the tip o'me tongue – Griffiths, that's it!' Some stared at me in deep suspicion.

'I am, I am!' I would bleat agitatedly, getting a bit shrill.

In order to project my image, to become known, I did a lot of after dinner speaking, danced with Commodores' Ladies – an ordeal for both, akin to Cornish wrestling – presented trophies and attended bow tie and gum boot regattas up creeks. We once attended a Class Rally.

All the visiting yachts were rafted up alongside so that people could wander at will from boat to boat and admire the additions and alterations wrought down below by inventive owners. 'Perhaps you'd like to see where I've stowed my little octahedral?' one invited shyly. A treat of this calibre was not to be passed over lightly. I showed him my loo seat retainer, a boon to men on port tack. Children crawled and peered like miniature planning inspectors. Joyce was below getting lunch ready. She became aware of a row of eyes at the coachroof windows. 'Ugh!' said a disparaging voice, 'jam doughnuts! *We've* got summer pudding.'

'Sod off!' I hissed, smiling disarmingly.

The day ended hideously with a sing-song. We all crowded aboard the Commodore's boat, the largest or at least the beamiest, where a single Party-Pak tin of beer was produced. We were all as sober as Circuit Judges. Liquid was dispensed sparingly into mugs.

'Well, cheers all!' said the Commodore hollowly, raising his. Then, as if making an announcement, he cleared his throat and pitched his voice, 'Old MacDonald had a farm'.

'Eee-eye-eee-eye-Ooooo!' the congregation sorrowed dutifully.

I wasn't getting much sailing in, apart from boat tests and press day demonstrations of new equipment, such as the new diesel outboard motor. Ten journalists in ten dinghies, adrift on a rainswept gravel pit, jerking starter cords. Eight engines remained mute. There were free ballpoint pens, brochures for all, and a harassed PR desperately plying us with drink.

Weekends, Bank Holidays and an annual week or ten days didn't leave me much time for voyaging to where the flying fishes play, but there was always the North Sea where Captain Cook and Lord Nelson started. They had to start somewhere.

17

Creeks and freebies • Two to a bag • Sabbaticals • Knock-down

The southern North Sea, the 'narrow seas', is the same colour throughout, an opaque dun-browny-grey. Whether in thirty inches or as many feet or fathoms (metres are Napoleon's Revenge) the colour gives no clue. In the far west or the south, water colour cannot be ignored. In the southern North Sea you watch the ripples, heed the slicks and swirls, listen for the dry rustle of shoaling water, and beware.

At first I feared the shallows, allowing ten feet over every bank despite drawing only three, but in time I became a creek-crawler like the rest. My first boat had an echo-sounder, a huge early model. When it packed up I hove the guts out and used it as a stowage for my hand-lead.

One of the great delights was to carry a young flood tide up some shoaling creek, 'touch-and-go', keel nudging, sticking and going on again the way the bargemen did it. Everything got plastered with mud. We found 'holes' where you could lie afloat at low tide, moored fore-and-aft. We all had our favourite holes. The challenge came when somebody beat you to it.

I set up my own secret leading marks on the mud: a twig in there lined up with a bottle on a stick, a tussock of grass in transit with a distant building. I'd come barrelling in, let go my kedge astern, bring up, let my bower go, and middle on both. Some son-of-a-bitch altered them. We spent a night on our earhole.

Solitude was the prize. Being entirely cut off. A man in a small motor cruiser followed me into one of my holes. I anchored; so did he. I settled to wait for the ebb. He called over, frowning, puzzled.

'What's 'ere mate?'

'Bugger-all,' I said helpfully.

'Oh,' he said, getting under way again, getting stuck.

Most of my pilotage was centred around the 'reduction to soundings' sums, designed to tell you the least depth to expect in your anchorage. They seldom worked out. A strong nor'westerly which stuck in the northern North Sea brought up a storm surge and raised the tides. In the magazine we gave away free cardboard devices of great ingenuity and even greater complexity, purporting to solve the problem. Readers bumped and cursed. I entered a river on one occasion looking for an anchorage, my echo-sounder giving a blurry signal. There was a similar-size yacht at anchor with a man in the cockpit. I yelled out.

'Excuse me, what water have you please?' There was a whispered conversation down the hatch.

'Not a lot,' he said, 'but we can spare you a kettle full.'

Sailing the North Sea, making for Ostend or the Westerschelde, was nerve-racking if, like us, you'd ever been run down. It is a hazy place where tides of unpredictable strength are subject to storm surge. You sail with eyes screwed up searching for buoys and beacons, vague motes that can mean safe or sorry. All the while, ships are passing. Not ships, they look like a bit of dockland gone to sea – huge, square, lumbering and shapeless.

Long weekends meant Ostend. One visit we made was harrowing. It was the usual North Sea murk and a troublesome dead run in a four to five and gusting. We took the usual course; Swin, Sunk, Galloper, thence to the West Hinder, scene of my belt on the head long ago. The first shipping lane athwart our course came up late in the afternoon, a ten-mile total with a Tom Tiddler's separation zone halfway, the first lane southbound, the second lane north. There wasn't much traffic. Sometimes there isn't and at others the ships are bunched bow-to-stern and staggered. For a yacht crossing square at maybe five knots this means trying to nip tight under the stern of the first in order to cross the bows of the next.

It isn't always possible if the second ship is well *beyond* the first. Do you then duck around her stern as well? Do you open the cocks and try to get across? While you agonise, a third and fourth great shape is manifesting through the gloom. What yachts are not allowed to do is deviate from that right angle course across the lanes. You can cross a ship or go *with* her. Otherwise it is all on the throttle, dry of lip and popping of eye. We saw one Panamanian stern-down and with a string of grey washing out aft. The second lane was no different. Then we were across; it was six o'clock so we got the gin out and had our one snort of the day.

The next separation system is narrower, a couple of miles only. It was dark by then, and West Hinder lightship was flailing its beam around. You feel stark naked. Then to port there arose a mammoth shape speckled with lights. It blew a terrible roar at us and charged past, clanking into the murky night. I thought, 'Sod this, should I turn and go back?'

There was no choice to be made for there was another Goliath behind us now, materialising like a print in the developer, a nightmare, her bulbous bow parting the sea in a sleek black flume. I felt the first sick touch of panic. I drew a deep breath and tried to whistle. It came out as a gulping sigh. The beam of light suddenly sprang upon us – not the Hinder, another light. It clawed over our sails, studied us fore and aft, fixed upon me at the helm rendering me blind and helpless. A metallic foreign voice crackled unintelligibly. I couldn't see a bloody thing. We were enclosed in a bubble of hard, white brilliance. I waved it away in vain.

It stayed. From beyond it came rushings and clankings, sirens bellowed, there came waves that hissed and broke, but always that great glare of light fixed upon us. I could do nothing; I just followed the compass heading and hoped that somebody knew what the hell he was doing – this mercantile guardian angel who spoke Dutch or Walloon or French at us.

Then the light left us and we groped in the darkness, rubbing eyes that still saw sparks and Will-o-the-Wisps. I looked at the echo sounder and found that we were safe now from big ship threat, even though I had no idea where we were. I hove-to and started hunting for and timing lights.

At breakfast time we berthed in Ostend by the Yacht Club and alongside a small motor/sailer with a tiny mainsail like the vestigial thumb of a horse. A man sat on her deck nursing a pint mug of morning tea.

'Just got in then have you?' he asked agreeably, a man of perception.

I told him of our adventure in the shipping lanes.

'Lane? We never seen no lane. What sort of lane?'

'It's a buoyed channel.'

'We never seen no buoys. I tell a lie; we *did* see a buoy, only it had foreign writing on it so we took no notice.'

As a yachting journalist I had learned about 'freebies'. A manufacturer sends you, unsponsored, a sample of his product in the expectation that you will try it and then fall about in rapture and write glowingly in the magazine. Having had his free plug he might even buy advertising space. You never *asked* him to send it. You are in no way committed. On the other hand, and in the interest of readers, you have a duty to try it.

I received everything from a luminous hat to a herb pillow 'for a deep and dreamless slumber'. Slumber aboard boats is ordinarily a non-stop nightmare engendered by the sound of wind and water. Fearsome phantasmagoria drag you erect with a wild cry. You hit your head and slump back groaning. 'Herb pillows indeed!'

The first 'breathable fabric' brought a one-piece sailing suit that breathed seawater, and I ended up wearing plus fours full of it. The 'Survival' suit came next; it was a spin-off from the oil rigs (everything was either Space Project or Oil Rig). I leapt into a swimming pool and surfaced feet first, which was where the air ended up.

The first Pot Noodle vied with high energy (Space Project) Malted Milk and a novel pan which automatically made porridge to perfection; Kendal Mint Cake battled with glucose pellets and what looked like edible chipboard – or was it a DIY sample?

Colin Jarman proving something or other. His moustache
dripped permanently like a wishing well grotto.
He is not happy.

Then there was 'Mannihose', tights for men. I had a midwinter freebie trade trip to Sweden due – the perfect trial. I eased myself into them, caught the train, plane and transfer coach – all of them as hot as the Arabian Gulf, like the hotel lobby and the nightclub to which our hosts whisked us away on the corporate buttering-up exercise. By then I was glowing crimson, and jets of steam were spurting out of my ears. I was near to collapse. A doctor was summoned by solicitous hosts who could do nicely without a stiff on the books.

'Ee wear too much cloths!' he diagnosed brilliantly.

There was a cheapie fire extinguisher (a Pekinese could lift a leg more effectively), and a lifesaving gadget that fired a balloon skywards – we asked the manufacturers if we could choose ten at random for test. They backed off.

Then there was the boat burglar alarm. It was so cheap that everybody could afford one or even two. I phoned Portsmouth Harbour police. 'Yes,' they'd cooperate in a test. The manufacturers declined to attend. 'We have faith in our product,' they said smugly. They had booked whole-page advertising.

We installed it in a boat in the marina. The police sent along their breaking-and-entering expert who arrived with some very specialised equipment – a crowbar and a bloody great screwdriver. He sniffed around hatches and windows and skylight. 'Stand back please,' he said. First the padlock went flying, courtesy of a twist from his screwdriver. I was busy with my camera. 'Now, stand *right* back!' In a single movement he whammed the sliding hatch back and flattened the alarm just as it uttered one brief squawk. He'd guessed where he'd find it.

Our published report sent our reader-credibility soaring, reduced the ad manager to tears and got me a bollocking from the boardroom.

Press Days are an editorial plague. If you send your youngest, rawest staff member he/she is liable to come back to the office clutching a truckload of brochures, besotted with the product and half-sloshed, and, unless sat upon, eager to write two whole columns plus pics. Worse yet, the advertiser may take umbrage at you for sending along a junior.

Lured by the promise of an incredible breakthrough in design technology which was to be unveiled in an amazing and hitherto secret venue, I travelled to Birmingham to see massively boobed dolly-birds demonstrate a new deckchair.

I'd joined the magazine in 1966; now, four years later, understaffed and underfunded by the huge group that owned it I was under pressure. Nevertheless the magazine was growing, and I loved my job despite the daily commute. Southend – Liverpool Street station was no great hike, but I hated it fiercely. In winter trains were a hot frowst reeking of wet wool and Vic Vapour Rub. If you saw a vacant seat you took it at your peril. Your neighbour would turn a jowly, crimson face. 'Good bordig', it would greet you sorrowfully and infectiously. In summer it was aftershave, armpits and Nivea cream. We'd leave the coast when the first indigo bars of a faint breeze were striping the mauve horizon with the promise of a gorgeous day. We would return, jaded, sweaty and weary just as the sun was losing its glory.

I stepped off the train one day, tie loosened, crumpled and hot. There was a little grey man in a grey suit with a grey complexion. I said to him, 'today was a right bastard. If I didn't enjoy my job I'd chuck it in!'

He plodded, carrying briefcase and crumpled evening paper. 'I have commuted for the past forty years,' he replied slowly. 'I have *hated my job every day of it!*'

Joyce sent me off single-handing for long weekends just to unwind. No great voyages, just a few miles along the coast. You don't need to go far because single-handed sailing means forward planning, hunching, pricking the chart in advance, clearing the anchor cable for a snag-free drop, and all this is totally and diametrically opposite to the life of phones and memos.

Walton Backwaters was my usual destination. It is an area of creek and whispering marsh – in those days still unsullied by speed-boat and 'wet-bike'. I would anchor on a running-moor to my own private marks, plenty of way on, kedge warp snaking astern, bringing up solid, biting in hard while I galloped forward, let go bower, hauled aft. Then I could watch the tide ebbing away and the mud cliffs becoming exposed with little green crabs panicking.

So down the Swin and through the Spitway heaving my lead, up the Wallet and through the Medusa – named for Nelson's frigate and a gamble he took, a young man destined for great things.

'Great things' for me were anchoring in one of those 'holes' followed a Vesta packet freeze-dry supper. Happy as a pig in dung I would potter on deck, then out would come grandad's melodeon, a couple of tots of Glen-Tesco and my pipe.

You had to read the instructions on those Vesta meals – the 'Fisherman's Platter' and the 'Shepherd's Pie'. I would pore over them tipsily like an archaeologist deciphering runes. Then came the *coup de grâce* of a half-bottle of Côte de Tesco. I'd wake up in the sunset afterglow and wash dishes feeling ghastly but totally relaxed.

At high tide I often rigged the dinghy and sailed the serpentine guts and gullies of the saltings, marron grass hissing along my topsides, twist and turn, tack and run. In hot weather I sailed nude. One day the maze of channels brought me out into the main fairway. Yachts everywhere. I downed sail, covered my options with it and rowed. 'I'd hoist my sail if I were you,' a man said helpfully.

It was when I was coming back from one of those sabbaticals that I almost bought it. I was heading west through the West Swin, and the day was hot with no more than a whisper of a breeze; thunderheads were building their crazy cloud towers. They'd never have got planning permission. I had recently bought a big lightweight ghoster for such weather, and we rippled along at a couple of knots. Then the wind came ahead, faltered and died. The tide was almost done.

I should have borne off and kedged on the edge of the Maplin. I had a drying mooring to pick up off Leigh, and if I missed a tide I'd be late for work.

The boat had a two-stroke auxiliary. It was about as temperamental as a Royal Opera diva; the more urgently you needed it the more certain it was to muck you about. I needed it badly. There was a ritual, a 'form' to observe which was as unvarying as a holy writ.

First it was out plug, then dry points on seat of pants, in plug, and try again. Next you removed it again and 'pencilled' the points. Then you lit the cooker and, with pliers, held it in the flame, juggling with the dexterity born of desperation to screw it back in the engine. Finally, the unthinkable: you broke out your brand new, virginal, freshness-sealed spare plug.

Joyce once reduced me to sobbing frustration. I had just been through the whole routine without a flicker of life from the engine. She said, *incredibly*, 'The last time this happened it started when I opened the forehatch!'

I tried to breath slowly and deeply, fighting for control. I failed. 'Don't be so bloody ridiculous!' I howled.

She opened it. The engine roared into life. It makes you bitter.

I was basting the plug when I heard a rushing sound that got louder and louder, like a flock of birds ... then the boat went flat on her beam ends.

I'd had the sheets flattened in and belayed and the squall laid her flat with her rudder out of water and the cleated lee sheet deep under water, a torrent roared in through the open companionway, filling her to bunk level as I fought to get on deck. I hung on, trying to think. Knife. This was why we carried knives. I reached down and slashed. She came upright like an old dog shaking itself. Then the wind began to get up.

The impractical exercise • Life on the mud • 'Throw me back,' said Bill

An editorial office can be made to run like clockwork, and the magazine will be about as interesting as a health farm breakfast. You need excitement and a touch of chaos. Instead of assembling a staff of journalists I got together a crew of sailors who could string words together. We sat on one another's desks and debated, postulated and argued. 'What would happen if ...?' 'How do you catch a fly-away halyard, clear a prop, kedge off a lee shore?'

'What would happen if we hit a container. Could our bilge pump cope?' We went afloat and found out by opening seacocks and pulling the log impeller, measuring how much water rushed in and whether the pump coped. It didn't. We got down to bucketing. They say a panicking man with a bucket beats any pump.

We called them 'Practical Exercises'. Our insurers never knew what we got up to. Could you hoist yourself aloft by running the engine flat out ahead, while towing a big bucket astern via snatch-block and tailed on to the halyard? No, we discovered, you couldn't. Can you get at a seacock by careening at anchor – masthead halyard to waterlogged dinghy alongside? Yes, you can.

Readers loved it and wrote in with technical suggestions such as 'what the bloody hell are you playing at?' We collected up their defunct flares and fire extinguishers, and took them to a testing range and fire station. Very chastening. A reader, on Guy Fawkes night, took his time-expired red star rocket into the kitchen to read the instructions. 'Pull tab.' He pulled it. There he was, prone, while this goddam thing tore around, up, down, in and out, ceiling to doormat, wrecking the Welsh dresser and putting the fear of God up the dog.

I explored the possibility of pumping up a dinghy from scratch while overboard and treading water. A reader who was a doctor specialising in hypothermia put the boot in. 'The man in the water is middle-aged and skinny, and he is soaked. Once in the dinghy he has no shelter from the wind. *He'll be dead by next morning!'* he wrote helpfully.

I was a bit obsessed by the man-overboard dilemma. My concern dated from just after the war when a mate of mine, old Paddy, had gone cross-Channel with three others in an old ex-Dublin Bay racer. On the way back the wind and sea kicked up. Paddy had been steering; he stood up to pee and overboard he went. Army great coat and boots – it was Easter and cold. They went round three times trying to get to him. The boat looked and behaved like a boomerang, long ends slamming down, never a hope. Paddy had long moustachios and was proud of them. They told me, guiltily, shamefully, *'He died looking comical!'*

Then there was a Fastnet Rock race. It started in a sou'westerly gale. In RORC races you always got your start; once across the line it was up to the skippers whether they sheltered or not. Nobody ever did. After a hell of a night we were heading inshore towards Brixham on port tack. I was on the wheel. A chap came up to empty the gash bucket (no environmental concerns back in the fifties). He let go of the coachroof grabrail in order to use both hands in rinsing it out, and he'd gone.

Paul (with cunning learned by bitter experience) is wearing a wetsuit for this lifting technique. He is not unconscious, merely in his dinner-hour.

I followed the drill. The drill takes over when your mind blanks out, which mine *did*. I yelled 'Man Overboard', threw the life ring and began the gybe. Then it all went wrong. An instant gybe brings you back to the man in the water, but it may bring you back *too soon*. There are better methods.

They poured up from below but there was a lee-guy on the boom; nothing was ready. The heaving line fell short, a kapok ring, saturated and sank ...

We went round again. The owner had the wheel and he overshot. Anybody might. Then round again. By now the man was drowning. It was on his face, an expressionless mask. Grey, dead-eyed, arms flailing. We got an end of a jib sheet into his hand. His fingers snapped shut on it. His face was underwater, distorted, but we had him.

What happened next is the crux of the whole man-overboard dilemma. It took six fit men nearly ten minutes to get him aboard. There is no room on a side-deck to use your strength, no room for more than two at a time to work. Unless you have made special provision for hauling up a waterlogged, exhausted casualty you will probably end with a tragedy. Now the most dreadful dilemma of all and the most common: a heavy husband and a diminutive wife! Think it over very carefully.

We worked it over until readers began to moan: men said their wives wouldn't sail with them, wives complained that *they* were consigned to the high-risk deck jobs (sensible), and nutty inventors came up with solutions that stopped just short of cork bras and exploding trousers. More dangerously, people began practising a 'man overboard' drill with a boathook and a couple of joined-up fenders. It is so far removed from the genuine emergency and the problem of hooking somebody out that it was a danger. 'We've got really good at it!' one lot told me at the Boat Show.

We went afloat and tried out every idea. 'Use the jib as a scoop' was one. OK if the jib is set 'flying' but not if it has to be unhanked, and worse still if it's on a roller. So, why not use the mainsail, run it out of its luff track, dump the belly overboard, get your bloke into it, then parbuckle him up? Let's try it, we said.

We had a thing going with an Accident Prevention Organisation. Ban the stepladder, outlaw the banana skin and put on your lifejacket before you get out of bed. We kept tongue-in-cheek; we invited them to send an observer.

We got this hearty, leathery lady in thick stockings carrying pamphlets. We called her (privately) Olive Oyle, after Popeye's

Yachting Monthly *man-overboard exercises with Bill 'throw-me-back' Beavis testing a lifesaving quoit with the resignation born of repeated dunkings.*

Bill being parbuckled in the mainsail, shortly before Olive Oyle threatened him with the Kiss of Life

girlfriend. Same tubular figure, same tubular skirt designed to remain an inch below the knee in force ten, although the prospect of it doing otherwise gave us little cheer.

Bill Beavis volunteered. Bill was destined to die young, but nobody forgets him. Somebody always had to go overboard on these stunts. Bill went in with a mighty splash, wailing loudly and threshing around in spectacular fashion. Olive Oyle was in her element, bounding around, getting in the way, taking photos and shouting encouragement to Bill.

The mainsail worked well, though how it would have fared in wind and sea is debatable. We got Bill into it and rolled him up and on to the side-deck, where he gave his special RADA interpretation of a cadaver – eyes rolled up and jaw sagging. 'Now then,' said Olive Oyle, 'I shall demonstrate the Kiss of Life!' Bill sat bolt upright. 'You bloody won't!' he cried, 'Quick, throw me back!'

The survival bag experiment earned me a blast from the boardroom. My behaviour was not what the company expected from its editors. It happened when Andrew Bray was my deputy editor. He was a very large young man, and I was no pixie in a little red cap.

After my gloomy experiment of inflating a dinghy while in the water a manufacturer sent us a freebie survival bag, a very large orange coloured plastic sack. 'It is better to have two persons sharing in order to pool body heat', read the instructions. What sort of 'two people'?

We were accommodated in a tower block of offices with Valhalla – the boardroom and top-brass dining suite – at the top. From time to time God-the-Chairman would descend and conduct VIP visitors on a tour of the magazines. Some expressed a wish to visit *Yachting Monthly*.

Andrew and I, with difficulty and much grunting and rolling around on the office floor, had finally managed to squeeze into the bag. The whole staff was on its feet and cheering us when the quality grey pinstripe walked in. There was a very long silence. A very long silence.

'THIS,' said God in a strained voice, '*is our editor!*'

I peered out, crimson-faced from exertion. 'Oh, hello!' I croaked. 'We're, ah, researching survival techniques!'

At the Boat Show and at a fat trade discount we bought a twenty-four foot GRP twin-keel Snapdragon cruiser and named her, with a whimsicality I now shudder to recall, *Miss-print*. Seen at the show, aground on a pile of polished pebbles and amidst the usual potted palms, she looked a taut little ship. Later, on the mooring off Leigh, she looked like a novelty soapdish. Joyce said, 'We should have called her *Miss-take*.'

In fact she was typical of the boats owned by many of our readers – our problems would be their problems, to be considered at length in future issues. We were to shuttle to and fro and around the southern North Sea in comfort and reasonable safety for the next three or four years, even if the sight of her failed to bring a lump of pride to my throat

Our daughter was able to bring a school chum along. The forward cabin had a door which they could shut to moan about us. Up with adolescence, down with parents. Michele was rising twelve and bursting out in all directions. The yacht club Cadet Officer, beefing about lifejackets, said, 'Look at Michele there. She's sensible. She's got hers on *underneath* her sailing smock.'

'Oh no I haven't!' Mitch said archly.

I learned a lot about twin-keelers. They're supposed to be shoal draught boats. Forget it. If you ground and stick top of the tide and on flat ground you stick like a clock on a mantlepiece. You can't heel them to reduce draft as you can with a keel-boat.

If you have a drying mud mooring though, you can sit there like an Indian Prince on an elephant while boats all around are on their ears. You can go out there and work, leaving your wellies on the mud alongside. You must attach them by little painters or the flood will sneak in. You'd see whole squadrons of boots under way, a stirring sight.

Ashore, anti-fouling twin keelers was no joke. Lying flat on your back means that you can't quite reach; if you kneel you get a barnacle-free scalp. I made a special little trolley with an adjustable back. I could whizz to and fro like one of those tragic beggars seen in Eastern bazaars. 'Poor devil!' people would murmur with compassion.

Only once did I use the keels when we brought up at anchor. It was in the mouth of Conyer Creek. We dried out on the sloping face of a mud bank, *athwart* the incline instead of up-and-down. The downhill keel was in a soft patch and it began. The water left us and the angle of heel increased.

'Nobody move!' I cried. 'Everybody uphill!'

The loo was on the downhill side. We'd filled buckets with water for flushing it but we had to empty them and use the buckets. We spent the evening perched like sparrows on a wall. I had a teaspoon on a string for use as a plumb-bob against the door frame. 'This is bloody ridiculous,' Joyce said, which it was.

We sailed in a Third World of yachting. In yacht havens and marinas, craft lay alongside at huge cost while owners stomped up and down in shorty yellow boots pushing trolleys. We wore wellies and squelched out over the mud to our mooring carrying things under arms, over shoulders or draped around necks. If your boots stuck you went down on your knees as though in supplication.

Or you could dry out against old motor tyres alongside ex-D-Day timber baulks. Alternatively there was 'Les's, a clangorous assortment of corrugated iron shacks out on the saltings where mud-berths could be arranged. You reached it via squirting duckboards and at high tide on tiptoe wearing thigh-boots.

A mud-mooring had to be allocated by the Foreshore Parks and Gardens Department. They would send a man who would stride mightily to and fro counting paces, then drive in a marker peg with a copper label for your chain – which in due course would develop an attack of galloping electrolysis.

Mooring sinkers of quality were concrete blocks specially cast, hollow-bottomed for suction. Dustbin lids used as moulds contributed an attractively fluted edge. Or an old flywheel, engine block or gas cooker could be employed. I had half a railway sleeper. I also had my 'mud suit', an old boiler suit condemned to hang on a nail at the back of the garage and regarded by Joyce with the particular loathing people reserve for spiders in the bath. Then you had to dig.

A mooring root digger is like an assassin clandestinely burying a corpse. The moment the tide recedes he digs a three-foot hole in concentrated panic, boots in the body and fills in the hole with the same haste to get done before the water returns. I favoured piling the spoil in a circular redoubt, thus buying a few extra vital minutes. You have to take up the riding chain in winter or somebody will nick it. Come the spring there is the ceremony of 'Looking for your Roots', hinting at a genealogical scrutiny of frail old documents and scraping moss off tombstones. You'll see solitary figures out there on the mud, heads bowed, apparently in mental anguish, pacing to and fro. 'Why not go talk to your parish priest, my son?' ask compassionate observers.

I loved all this, and I still do. It enriched my job. I could be mixing with millionaires and sailing their magnificent boats on Friday and mixing tar-and-cement on Saturday morning. Sailing from a mud-mooring was like a hark back to boyhood and the Hull boating lake, 'Coom on in number nine!'

With a 'drying mooring' you left your mooring as soon as your boat staggered to her feet; you dashed around in all directions for a couple of hours or so and then, like some gum-booted Cinderella, you hurried back to reach your buoy before the clock struck midnight and you stuck a hundred yards short of it – which meant an eight hour wait.

All this stuff filtered into the magazine, perhaps to the private disapproval of the Advertisement Department which preferred the editorial to court the well-heeled reader who had unlimited spending power, drove Land Rovers as second cars and whose wives wore mohair cardies. I was unrepentant; I was treading in the muddy footprints of Maurice Griffiths MC.

The white-stick sailors • 'Touch' and go • 'Is it dangerous?' Cathy asked

Replying to readers' letters is one of an editor's penances. The time to mourn, though, is when you don't get any. Readers' letters are the beating heart of a magazine, and you ignore them at your peril.

A reader told me, early on, that he had been a regular reader for forty years. 'I wrote to Griffiths with a query. He replied promptly, courteously and usefully. I have never forgotten it!' He had remained a reader ever since. I made it a rule that all letters were answered, all phone enquiries sorted, and if we didn't know the answer we *rang them back the same day*. It astonished people. 'Oh, I didn't *really* think you would!'

Some write because they are lonely, some because they enjoy bitching ... 'I was astounded, outraged, amazed to read, etc'. Some have genuine technical queries. There are those who are frustrated writers, and others who are bored. There are bra-burning women's libbers threatening the Press Council, and poor souls who have lost their marbles and write gibberish.

I replied to them all, some a bit curtly. One woman wrote objecting to our use of the word *seaman*ship and accused me of being a chauvinistic pig. I wrote back, 'Dear madam grunt-grunt. Yours etc.' Another, a male, was abusive and rude. I should have ignored him. I sent him a little drawing which showed an editor holding a smoking gun and a pair of up-turned feet. *Both wrote back in huge good humour.*

Then I started getting typed letters from a man in Wales who owned a Leisure 17, which is about as small a cruiser as you can get. You don't so much go on board it as 'put it on' like a hermit crab backing into a whelk shell. His name was Harold Hayes. Could he fit full-height guardrails and pulpits? he wanted to know, plus a great deal more. His letters kept on coming. Finally I wrote back listing a selection of reference books. 'Get your local library to order them for you,' I suggested, adding that I really couldn't go on replying to his letters.

'Dear Mr Sleightholme,' he answered, 'Don't I wish I could take your suggestion. The fact is that I am *totally blind* ...' I phoned him. He cruised his little boat with his wife and kids. They were his eyes. Everything else was up to him – the sailing and the decision-making. I felt awed and humble. At the weekend I went afloat alone, found a patch of open water and blindfolded myself. I discovered a totally new and exciting world that I had never suspected.

Standing at the tiller I felt the breeze against my cheek, the tiller pressure, the changing angle of heel and the multiple sounds of wind and water. I moved the tiller and *everything changed*! Sails rustled, heel increased, wind angle, tiller pressure and water sounds altered, and went on altering. Astonished, I wore off, luffed up, tacked and gybed while the signals poured into my mind, building up pictures, fresh dimensions.

I was all agog. Sailing for the Blind. Mental headlines raced through my brain. Here was something I could do. The magazine could be the tool. I began to plan a special sort of boat. I would beg a GRP hull shell, maybe a Westerly. Instead of a coachroof she would have a vast self-draining cockpit. She would have ropes of widely differing feel and texture, Braille labels everywhere and audio signals that squawked if anybody did something unsafe.

I phoned Harold. He heard me out. I had expected wild enthusiasm but instead received silence. It was the sort of uncomfortable silence you get when a diner drinks his finger bowl. Plainly I had boobed. Finally he spoke.

'Er-um!' he said. 'How can I put this. What we'd really like is an *ordinary* boat!'

I revised my plans and began phoning around among the various organisations for the blind and sight-handicapped. It was like trying to sell trousers to nuns. The Royal National Institute for the Blind was the only one to show interest, but they were cash-strapped and fully committed. Others thought that sailing was 'unsuitable', incurring needless risks. The Sailing Centre run by the Council for Physical Recreation opined that, 'We would never, never subject our instructors to such grave responsibility!'

Belatedly I tried the Royal Yachting Association Seamanship Foundation and struck gold. First I had to work for it. The Chairman was Owen Aisher. His PA said I could see him after breakfast in his London flat, which was a bloody nuisance since it meant catching a very early train.

He heard me out in silence and read my typed notes. Then he systematically tore my idea to shreds. You'd have thought he was going on a paperchase; he sneered, blasted my plans, derided them. 'Oh bloody forget it!' I burst out. 'Sorry to have wasted both our time.' I was at the door when he gave his characteristic double sniff and stopped me.

'I was making sure that you'd done your homework and thought it through properly. I like it. I shall give the Council my strongest recommendation to take it up!' Which for him was like cocking a double-barrelled shot gun. That happened maybe thirty years ago.

I didn't *invent* the idea; neither did Harold. Isolated cases of blind people going sailing were common enough, but I don't think there existed anywhere an organisation to promote it. Once the articles began to appear in *Yachting Monthly* there came letters from Canada, Germany, France, Switzerland, New Zealand and elsewhere, all from groups eager to know more.

The first sailing course took place in Poole, organised by Duggie Hurndall, courtesy of the Royal Motor Yacht Club and half a dozen family sailing cruisers with their owners. It lasted a whole week, and we learned as much as our pupils. They came from the RNIB, ages ranging from two young girls in their teens to middle-aged and older. What we instructors learned at once was that there is no such thing as 'the blind', a separate species. They are you and me with our eyes closed.

Sighted people struggle for words, trying to avoid words like 'let's see' or 'look at this'. Sightless folk use them all the time. People are just people.

I had an open two-seater sports car. I nipped into a shop leaving a girl sitting on a young man's knee. When I came back he had a red handprint across his chops.

'... after all,' he was saying, blushing and repentant, 'it was only like I was reading a sort of Braille!'

'Let's go into a shop,' said Tony, blind from birth and with a malicious grin. We went into a chemist to buy suntan cream. Tony said what he wanted loudly and clearly. The shop assistant instantly turned to me. She said, 'Does he want the larger size?' Tony spluttered.

That week was wonderful. We had two students and four sighted crew on each boat. We'd planned to begin by 'showing' our students around on deck and below, for which we had allowed a full two hours. We were all under way within half an hour.

'Mental image,' our pupils explained. Tell us clearly, let us touch and we'll build up our own picture. It may not be what you'd think of as a boat, but it's *our* boat!' Harold had said this. He heard talk of how ugly modern container and bulk carrier ships had become. He'd smiled. 'I'm the lucky one then. I see ships with graceful lines the way I remember them.'

I had made up a Meccano tactile steering aid for each boat: a stern-pulpit-mounted wind vane and a length of speedometer cable were connected to a small, robust pointer that clipped to the tiller. The helmsman kept one finger on it. As the apparent wind direction altered and as the boat luffed or bore off the pointer recorded it. They worked beautifully but broke down constantly.

We found that steering on the wind was easy to grasp but running and reaching were difficult. People could sense the direction of the sun as a directional reference. Every job was tackled, from hoisting and stowing sails to putting in a reef in a squall. Safety harnesses got tangled up like a Maypole dance. There was a lot of laughter. On the last day it was on us.

Friday night. We didn't know why our students were going around grinning and whispering. In our total stupidity we instructors just didn't guess. We wanted to give our pupils the 'full sailing experience'. Friday night was to be it.

A blind sailing student getting in a tangle and finding it vastly funny. Without thinking, as a treat and a 'new experience' we took them for a night sail!

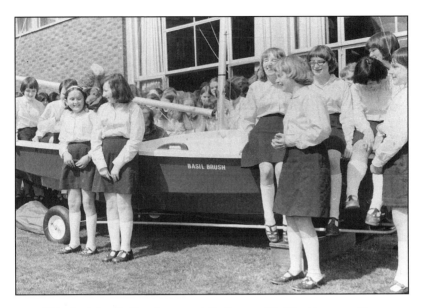

Blind girls of Chorleywood College with Wayfarer sailing dinghy Basil Brush *which they named after their favourite character (he's looking over the shoulders of the two little girls on your left). They learned to sail by ramming the banks of a gravel pit, guided by a sound beacon.* Yachting Monthly *readers bought the boat.*

They grinned and grinned. 'We're looking forward to this!' they said. Later, after sailing around in the blackness we were heading back, sidelights on, everything ashore all a-twinkle. They took pity and explained. 'Well that was really, really fascinating,' Tony said. 'I mean just imagine it, *sailing in the dark*!'

I knew that it was wrong for my magazine to plug too hard because it meant that rival titles would simply shun the subject of blind sailing, and it needed publicity. I was personally committed though. My last plug was to raise money from readers to buy a Wayfarer sailing dinghy for the blind girls of Chorleywood College. The kids named her *Basil Brush*, their favourite character. The creator of this animal even brought it along for them to stroke. I was a bit bloody choked.

Privately I took blind friends sailing in our own boat. One weekend, with two girls aboard, we anchored up the muddiest of creeks and, at low tide, virtually land-locked, I turned them adrift in the dinghy. Both were brilliant swimmers. With a sound beacon (radio on deck) they splashed around, helpless with laughter and covered in mud.

Another time I had a young chap on the helm. I left him sailing hard on the wind while I went below to the loo. I heard a rush of bow-wave. I hadn't noticed the other boat. I panicked, rushed on deck.

She was the port tack boat and just diverting around our stern. 'Morning,' said her helmsman.

'Morning,' said ours, blind from birth, grinning. Whoever he was, he never knew what fun he'd given my crew!

It isn't easy to find boat owners who are willing to offer berths to blind sailors – that is apart from the dedicated few who lend boats and time to the instructional courses. There are those who do it once then dine out on the anecdotes for the next ten years. The problems are not aboard the boat but from the sheer sweat in collecting and later delivering to people. Apart from the courses, I opted out leaving it to Duggie Hurndall who had the enthusiasm of ten men. I drove staff in the office crazy by making tactile scratch charts instead.

Without a chart, going out sailing is, quote, 'like heading out into a void'. Blind sailors need that vital mental picture that gives angles and distances relative to a starting point. You place a sheet of acetate over a chart and with the point of a needle raise a roughened trace of coast, land, rocks etc, with buoys punched to raise a pimple. The sound of scratching, hour after hour and in company time, drove my team frantic, teeth on edge and breathing bloody rebellion. They called it 'scritching'. 'God, he's at it again!' they prayed. I scritched at home, and Joyce delivered ultimatums; I scritched on the train and had a seat to myself.

Derek Fawcett, inventor and manufacturer of the Autohelm self-steering system, became involved and produced an 'audio' compass which became the nub of all sailing for blind helmsmen. While on course there was silence but wander off course, port or starboard, and you heard a high note, or a low one, which began with a slow beep ... beep, increasing beep, beep, beep, finally to a frenetic beepbeepbeep.

Students could steer the yacht by the hour, provided they had a lookout. 'It's like having your head in a bloody beehive', said one. They had a genuinely *useful job to do*. My secret regret was that my wind-vane was forgotten; we had human autopilots who could ignore wind direction.

Year by year we had courses in Thorney Island, Poole, Plymouth, Falmouth and elsewhere. They were huge fun. There was a 'touchy-feely' session with models, then straight afloat. We had a beginner section, a day-cruising group and the old hands who went foreign. Laughter was the common denominator.

Somebody got the idea of pairing off one totally blind with one partially-sighted person in their shore lodgings. Harry, a laconic Yorkshireman, told me one morning, 'Hey, that were a bloody daft idea. I asked my mate where the loo was. Silly booger only put me in a broom cupboard!'

Harry had lost his sight in middle age. He took up javelin-throwing with his son as his 'eyes'. They went out on the sports ground. First shot and he stuck it in the rugby goal crossbar. He wanted to try shot-putting. 'No bloody way!' his son told him. 'Try marbles, dad.'

Like many other sightless people, Harry had a fund of stories no sighted person would ever dare to tell. Like the one about the blind man who tried parachuting. 'Incredible!' people said. 'Simply amazing, but tell me one thing: how do you know when you're about to hit the ground?'

'Easy. The dog's lead goes slack!'

We were leaving the Plymouth marina one afternoon, me guiding Harry back to where I'd left my two-seater MGB parked on the quayside. He said, 'Des, are there many trippers up there?'

'Dozens,' I told him.

'Are you wearing sunglasses and are you game for a laugh?'

'Go on', I said.

'Right. You take my white cane. We're *both* blind, get it?'

I got it. Leading each other we weaved to and fro, teetering on the edge of the catwalk, bumping into bollards, finally mounting the ramp up to the dockside, me tapping away with Harry's cane, bumbling around. People rushed to our aid.

'Thank's just the same but we're OK,' Harry told them graciously. I found the car. We got in. I started the engine ... .

'Are the boogers scattering?' Harry asked. Oh yes they scattered. 'Ee, I really would like to see that!' he mourned.

One incident sticks out in my mind that summarises the whole ethos of this sailing for the blind business. It happened at the end of a cross-Channel cruise for more advanced students. We were homeward bound in Derek Fawcett's fine yacht. It was just before dusk and we were entering the shipping lanes, sailing fast and free.

I had the watch with young Cathy beside me, blind from birth but an ardent young sailor. She was steering by audio-compass. The thunderstorm had been hanging around for the past hour, rumbling and muttering; now, suddenly it struck.

There was an almighty bang and simultaneously a jagged flash; it was right over us. The rain and wind arrived together and we took off. Visibility closed to a yacht's-length, which in one of the world's busiest shipping lanes was scant comfort. There was another shattering bang. Cathy was having her work cut out to stay on course.

'Des, is this dangerous?' she said, head cocked, hands busy with the wheel.

'Oh no. Just a bit noisy!' She steered in silence for a bit. 'Come on, don't soft-soap me.' I said, 'OK then. Yes, if you want the truth, yes, it's bloody dangerous!'

'Well I'm glad,' Cath said. 'All my life I've been protected and fussed and shielded from everything nasty. Now this is *real*, I'm scared and I'll treasure it for the rest of my life!' So said young Cathy, blind but with a right to feel danger like the rest of us.

20

A cruising butty • Hanky-panky • A visit from the Mafia

During my nineteen years as editor the magazine changed ownership three times as one big publishing fish gobbled another. We also changed offices, from the creaking Edwardian elegance of Southampton Street to Hatton Gardens with its diamond cutters and nearby Covent Garden where cabbages were king, to a stiflingly hot suite in Stamford Street. Andrew rigged up huge fans from his father's chicken battery. We feared bumble-foot.

In Hatton we shared with an obscure religous journal whose editor was a time-expired old hack, serving out his last month. His staff included more dog collars than Crufts and enough black twill for a state funeral.

'Pious buggers,' he confided, whispering. 'I could make this rag a best-seller!'

'How?'

'Choirmasters, unfrocked priests, raped nuns!' he hissed, revealing his masterplan. He kept a bottle of Old Grouse in his desk; he could whip it out, take a snort and have it back at the rattle of his doorknob.

Our final office was twenty-two storeys up in a tower block housing IPC magazines of every sort. You could share a lift up with the twinset and tweed to *Country Life*, ride down with the cloth cap and khaki satchel from *Anglers' Mail,* or travel with *New Musical Express* which meant green mohican hairdo and ponchos of black dustbin liner.

This cohabitation of titles had its advantages. We held a 'Cruising butty' competition. Readers sent in sandwiches of their own invention, and we got *Woman's Own* to stage the judging. Andrew and I munched our way through eighteen while the cookery editor tapped one finger and looked at her watch. The winner was The Single-hander: a flute of bread sliced fore-and-aft, filled with bacon and egg at one end and marmalade at the other. A whipping held it together – you unwound as you proceeded. We burped.

'You've hardly touched that corned beef dog!' Joyce accused at supper.

We revelled in zany ideas. Most readers entered into the spirit of things; a few were outraged and said so at the Boat Shows. You could spot them bearing down on the stand, white about the lips, rehearsing the blast they were to deliver. We dared to poke fun and take the mick.

Dear old Bill Beavis had started it with his 'Polyestermite' – an entirely fictitious insect of his invention, a mutation that lived on fibreglass. Consternation swept the boatbuilding industry and yachting establishment. An eminent Research Laboratory in America pressed for photos and specimens. Bill was invited to address a special seminar; he had to kill it and fast.

Encouraged, I invented 'The Rollo Floating Anchor'. We published a fake photo. It looked like a garden lawn roller with flukes. Made of hard-wearing plastic it was a spin-off from the offshore oil industry. A one-way valve allowed it to be filled with water, thereby making it heavy. On recovery you simply drained it to lighten it again.

The buyer from a massive Canadian chandlery bought a copy of the magazine at Heathrow airport, while en route for home. He broke his journey and rushed into our office.

'I wanna be first, I wanna franchise!' he demanded.

He was certainly the first. Next came our April First Portable Echo Sounder. There was an echo sounder transducer knocking about in the office, complete with its coil of cable, ready to be fitted to my boat. We took it afloat and took a photo of a member of staff in the act of swinging it prior to taking a sounding like a traditional lead-line.

'Lightweight, completely portable, accurate ...' our caption proclaimed. We gave Paul's home number. 'Never stopped bloody ringing,' Paul grieved.

Andrew wrote a thing about the 'Auto-Cruiser' that won worldwide interest. 'Why get cold and wet? Why not send your boat cruising without a crew?' It was radar-guided, auto-steered, and electronically located.

Stop

Drain valve

Flukes

'The proposal *sickens* me!' roared venerable veterans with fingers missing from frostbite, standing in pools of water.

We adapted the classic Hoffnung barrel-of-bricks joke, representing it as a method for climbing aloft. 'First hoist aloft a weight exceeding that of the climber's body as a counterbalance ...' We issued hefty disclaimers. To our huge joy the idea was used in *Reeds Nautical Almanac* for real and for several years in succession.

There wasn't a hell of a lot to choose between our barmy inventions and our serious lines of research. I had this theory about windspeed. Why couldn't it be measured simply and cheaply by holding up a handkerchief by two corners and observing its flapping behaviour in an increasing wind?

There was a long, straight, country road and my two-seater convertible with the top down. Andrew stood up as if taking the salute. He had his handkerchief clutched by two corners. With an eye on the speedo I drove at 5–40 mph, ranging up and down the scale, calling out speeds.

Traffic overtook us or was overtaken. Laughingly drivers swerved and braked, plainly entering into the fun of the thing to judge by their cheery waves. The experiment was inconclusive.

There was a test lab in Southampton, and it had a wind tunnel. They would be glad (they said) to share my research into Handkerchief Behaviour in Varying Wind Forces.

I took along my then secretary, Julie Bickford, to take notes. I climbed into the wind tunnel. A man in a white coat eyed me oddly. There was bare standing room in the tunnel. I turned my rump to the fan, extended my handkerchief sideways and nodded. I was soberly dressed in sports jacket, slacks, shirt with club tie – nothing ostentatious.

The fan went 'Ohhhhhhhhhhh'. Force 1–3. Lazy undulations.

'Whooooooo,' Force 4–6. Undulations became flaps, increasing to a crackle.

My sports jacket rose over my head, shirt-tail shot out ... 'Wheeeee,' Force 6–Gale 8, trousers shot up legs, club tie flailing, Airtex vest

159

in motion and fishing smacks making for harbour. I broke into a trot. I think that I can say the experiment was a complete success. Julie and the man in the white coat were deeply and emotionally moved. They had tears in their eyes.

Foreign travel went with the job. Travelling to some fever-haunted clime to admire something, write about it and help sell ad pages on the strength of it was part of an editor's job. Politicians kiss babies, missionaries save souls and editors beam and nod.

There was a press trip for European editors to a mogul boat-builder in Florida, massive export pending, massive advertisement revenue likely and all of us beaming and nodding like car-back-window Plutos. Special charter flight and champagne with your cornflakes. What was special, we were informed, was that this boat interior had been designed by an all-American top designer who had won awards for his originality eg a telephone kiosk, a vacuum cleaner and his toilets in Pan-Am jets. He was a lissom young man with a lavender turtleneck and ponytail. 'Space,' he lisped, 'I have created space down below!' He had 'conceptualised' his design in the marina and in the horizontal. There was nothing to stop an occupant being rattled around like a pea in a whistle.

The company was an offshoot of a subsidiary of a parent company which specialised in TV dinners. It was loud and lavish. For four days we were socked by sales plugs, boatyard tours, trips afloat and fed TV dinners. By the end all the party were gutted. Clutching their free gifts of Chucky Chicken Instant DEEEP Fry they caught the flight as scheduled, but I discovered that my ticket would be valid to the end of the week. 'Why not have a couple of days sightseeing?' I asked myself. I shouldn't have answered.

By bus I saw the Space Centre and the Everglades, where I saw an alligator. It also saw me and showed a matching lack of enthusiasm. I bussed to Petersburg to catch my shuttle connection to Nassau via Miami from whence the transatlantic charterflight was to leave. It was comic nose time.

The shuttle was cancelled and the next flight *might just* make it provided there was a really rapid turn around and 'have-a-nice-day-now!' Panic to recover my baggage, panic to reach the departure terminal. I scorched to a standstill at the barrier.

'Hold it, bud,' the man said. 'You gotta wait for 'em to dis-em-bark OK!' So a quick turn around meant that the shuttle could leave on 'skedool'. Great, up came the boarding ramp. Now come on folks, shake it about. The aircraft door opened.

There were twenty-five of them for heaven's sake! There were twenty-five blue-rinsed all-American Moms in wheelchairs. Sashes across mighty bosoms proclaiming a Mum's Convention of some sort. The Press was there, smile and wave, each goddam one smiled and waved.

'Come on, COME ON!' I panted through gritted teeth.

'Hey, don't they just tug at your heartstrings!' the gate-man said. The flight missed the Nassau connection by five minutes. I spent the night in a hotel, my room vivid with flashing neon signs, enlivened by police, ambulance, fire engine and doubtless blood bank sirens.

At Nassau airport a man in a sharp suit looked me over. I asked where my charter flight would be. His smile didn't vanish because he never had one, but a 'got-ya' look came over his face. 'In here, bud', he said opening a door. The door had FBI written on it.

Two more sharp suits gave me a real going over. They frisked me down. I wasn't carrying. They were, shoulder holsters. They phoned the boat factory for confirmation, consulted, frisked my baggage, consulted again and let me go. I asked them what the hell it was all about. The man behind the charter flight was a drug runner and now in the slammer. There would be no charter flight, OK. It was history and tough, bud.

Free again and bag-in-hand I toured the airport, little Bo-Peep, ticket in the other hand. What now? At that time credit cards were coming into vogue, but not for old Sleightholme though, a plain man and plain spoke, who called spades spades and whose word was his bond. Nay lad, no bits of plastic for honest JDS. I was also broke. It was four days before a carrier would agree to honour my ticket. I found a room-only doss and lived on coffee and doughnuts, and doughnuts and coffee.

The BA flight took me to Luxembourg. I phoned my office; somebody had to buy me a ticket to London. There was a lot of interference on the line; it was bloody laughter. Meanwhile there was the coffee shop. And doughnuts.

Freebies that went sour were not confined to me alone; Andrew had his share. There was a Press and Boatbuilders Conference in Denmark. There had been a boat-review that had brought him into conflict with a builder who invoked legal big guns, swearing horrific revenge upon the magazine and Andrew, and demanding a rewrite and heads on platters. He and Andrew were on the trip together.

They had avoided each other like stalkers in 'injun' country. Sod's Law was involved, against which there is no defence. The hotel had cocked up the bookings. Single rooms had become doubles. Question: who shall share with whom? A Dane in a dicky read from a list. 'Meester So-and-so with Meester Such-and-such.'

Andrew, a realist, stared fixedly ahead. So did the boatbuilder. It surprised neither when, right at the bottom of the list, their names were called out. Together they rode the lift in silence. They reached their double room. *It had a double bed.*

For a cock-up on the heroic scale I had an Italian boatyard tour in the company of editors from both sides of the Atlantic. We were to visit ten boatyards in six days. By the time every son-of-a-bitch boatyard in the land had muscled in on the act we were sometimes doing six in a day.

Our coach driver was in a state of constant fury. With the horn blaring, a dust cloud astern and cursing peasants leaping with an agility born of a love of life, we raced from south to north and back again. Seldom did we reach our hotel before 1am (on one occasion it was almost 3am) then dining and bedding down at cock-crow.

At every stop, at every venue, there was a 'special finger-kissing local pasta'. We groaned and slobbered. A Swede went berserk. He'd invited us to his room for a last, *LAST* nightcap. His room gave onto a sheer eight-storey drop to the lobby. He had been silent, as though in deep thought. Suddenly he let out a terrible roar. 'Pasta, pasta, gut-dam PASTA!' he cried, leaping to his feet. He flung his bottle straight through the window. Down, down it sailed to shatter on the marble fountain.

The party broke up in haste. 'Bottle? What bottle? We never saw no bottle.'

He and I devised a game. Every boat we were shown seemed to be a ski-boat runabout. Simulated plastic mahogany trimmed with gilt and purple stripes.

The scam was for me to start peering up into an inaccessible locker, then straighten up frowning, beckon Sven who would also peer and frown. We would discuss heatedly, have a final peer and then walk away shaking our heads. It never failed. As soon as we had gone, down would come the Company Top Brass who would peer and frown.

In Naples the local Mafia did our coach. It was plainly a fix. The driver went for a leak, nod, nod, wink, wink. They took every camera bag and the entire stock of exposed film which meant that the whole exercise was invalidated. Just so many pasta-miles.

In an attempt to lift our spirits, despite it being midwinter and nearly midnight, we were given a quicky tour of the Pompeii ruins. Not the whole lot, just the naughty room with the graffiti. It was a game attempt, but the Naples police blew it.

'Never fear, you'll have your cameras back,' they promised hollowly, seating us in a large, bare room at HQ. 'Now signori some details!' This was more like it - action, these boys wouldn't muck around. We were given forms to fill in. Pages of details, who, what, when, where? Parentage? 'Name and religion of grandmother/grandfather/ ...

The Swede flipped his lid again.

21

A costly freebie • Thank you emu • The confessional • No star to steer by

You might be a good omelette cook or a good juggler, or mediocre at both, but never be a clumsy juggler of eggs. Likewise, if you are a halfway decent editor don't try to be a travel courier as well. Which was where I went wrong, although it was not of my choosing. There was a respectable travel agency that specialised in unusual world tours. You could choose from a selection: Live Steam which covered steam railways around the globe, a cricket tour, an angler's tour, an art tour and now, in 1971 a yachting tour.

It was also magazine promotion. For regular readers a special price of five hundred quid all-in (almost) for a month-long tour taking in Hong Kong, Australia, New Zealand, Fiji, San Francisco and home. Our publishers leapt at it. We were to have Sir Alec Rose as titular leader, me as a living embodiment of *Yachting Monthly*, a courier and forty lucky readers. All I would be expected to do was show my face. Like a sniper's target.

There was a preliminary get-together in London where everybody beamed at everybody else and nibbled sausages on little sticks. In mid-January we met again at Heathrow for the first night flight, destination Hong Kong. I wore my best yachting jacket with the hoss collar neckline.

Where was the courier? A lady courier had set up the whole tour, devised the route, contacted the yacht clubs en route, made the bookings, arranged the transfers.

The minute hand on the big clock gave another jerk. I was beginning to get an all-too-familiar feeling; I had been here before. Custard pie time folks. Then up raced a flustered little man holding a wodge of papers and folders.

'Ah!' he said, identifying his patsy. Me. 'Mister Sleightholme I presume.'

It was not an original line. He hitched his mouth corners up in a ghastly smile. 'A slight problem, I'm afraid, but nothing that can't be handled.' He shoved the wodge into my hands.

'Tickets, itinerary, bookings. Everything you need. Everything has been taken care of. All you have to do is enjoy the tour, and,' he added, fatally, 'if you have any doubts about *anything whatsoever,* just ring us.'

Our courier was having a nervous breakdown. I was IT. Ding-dong they were calling our flight.

Had I any doubts? Would I be able to ring the tour company? Would I hell-as-like. Even as we droned over France, poking around at our in-flight veal cutlets in synthetic gravy the Great National Postal Strike was getting into its stride. Every phone line into the UK was to be jammed solid.

The arrangement was that we would stay in luxury hotels but on a *room-only* basis, the tour brochure stated so clearly in 4-point type – which is the size you'd use for printing The Lord's Prayer on a postage stamps. We booked into the Peninsular Hotel, one-time favourite of Empire Builders, Agatha Christie and so on. Which was when the penny dropped.

The whole party fell upon me and verbally disembowelled me. 'Where would they eat? They hadn't budgeted for food!'

Next day one of the women was bitten by a child. ('I tried to pat the little bitch!') The day after that a man who'd ordered the twenty-four-hour tailoring job had his jacket split a seam from collar to bum. It was my fault on both occasions. At the airport prior to flying out, two of them refused to relinquish their passports to me for bulk processing, and we came near to missing the flight.

In Sydney we visited the yacht club to meet the members who had offered the chance of a sail next day. Sir Alec had been borne off in triumph to a dinner. We were heading back to the Hilton Hotel in a coach and I was on the public address mike, reading out who was going to sail in what and with whom. There was a catamaran.

'I tell you straight,' griped one lovable old reader, all his own teeth at sixty, own appendix *et al*, 'I refuse to sail in one of those things!' Another man said, 'Hear, hear, quite so.'

I flipped. I'd had enough. I said so at full volume. The coach had stopped at lights mid-city. Outside on the pavement a group of Oz supporters gave me a rousing cheer.

The visit to a zoological garden and aquarium included sharks and free-range emus. I wished the sharks had been free-range but pipe dreams, pipe dreams ... It started raining. An emu, a scraggy, six-foot tall bundle of stinking feathers, leaned over the shoulder of one of my charges and ate the lens-cap off his camera. It then let fall a gigantic greeny-yellow turd into which a lady placed her open-toed sandalled foot. You can always find consolation in simple blessings. Going back on the coach I was collecting for a tip for the driver. 'No,' said this berk, '*I shall decide,* not you!'

In New Zealand (Hilton) the sail-with-the-locals plan was thwarted; our courier had missed the fact that our visit coincided with a national holiday weekend. Local owners had their own arrangements, and they didn't include forty Limeys. I day-chartered a huge motor-sailer with room for all; the hotel agreed to do packed lunches, a fiver a head inclusive of champagne.

'No way!' came the universal howl. They weren't paying for champagne! *Five quid*!? Was I mad? At ten o'clock that night, I found a backstreet café where they'd make up forty no-nonsense, egg-and-cheese butties plus bun-and-Tizer for a couple of quid a head.

I retired to a bar, frustrated, very lonely, but determined not to let my magazine down. There was this *proper* tour courier on a tall stool.

'How many in your party?' he asked unprompted.

'Forty.'

'Well that means you've got four right bastards then.'

'How the hell did you guess?'

'I didn't,' he said. 'That's the usual, one-in-ten.'

At 2am a woman phoned my room. She'd lost her smalls in the wash.

'Well I sure as hell never took them!' I told her, slamming the phone down.

It was lonely because all the rest were in pairs. Nobody ever included me in their plans. Sir Alec was always whisked away to be fêted – or he was in his room quietly getting socko. He was a lovely old man.

One day when the doeskin jacket brigade from the yacht club came to collect him, he was not to be found. I found him though. He was down in the basement bar with a starry-eyed young man who wanted to cruise the world. Alec was saying '... Oh no you don't need a squaresail, although ...' It seemed wicked to break it up.

On regatta day I sat on the seawall, alone, to watch the racing. A parson in a dog collar came over; he was a Maori. 'On your own? Come with us.' There was a big launch packed with Maoris and canned ale. They were there to cheer the war-canoe race. They were the mums, dads and baby sisters of the canoeists who, they explained, had been practising for weeks sitting astride a wooden form in the church hall. We all waved our tinnies and yelled 'Pakia, pakia!' or something like that as the huge canoes tore by. It was a grand sight, and they were a grand bunch of folk.

We had a three-day stop in Fiji where Sir Alec and I underwent the 'Kava' ceremony in a village; local businessmen in loincloths and sharks' teeth officiated with solemnity. One morning I asked a taxi driver to take me to a secluded beach, any beach where my charges were not. He dumped and left me. It was secluded all right; there wasn't a soul to be seen – just a sweep of coral sand with a scuff of coconut palms and limpid water 80°F in temperature. I swam deep, then saw a monster clam shell open for business and surfaced. A man was shouting and waving. I waved back. He began to dance up and down so I went ashore.

'We *never* swim here. This bay is alive with sharks!' He made graphic munching jaw movements. Nothing else had gone wrong in Fiji, but at least I was *trying*.

It was to be a night departure for the long hop to San Francisco. It was time for another mindless cock-up. We took taxis to the airport and assembled on the main concourse. I counted heads and baggage. During the trip the baggage count differed at every stage as people bought extra bags or stuffed one inside another, but heads remained constant. Until now. I was two short.

Nobody had seen them. The big clock gave another jerk. Half an hour to lift-off. Where the bloody hell where they? I had women check the ladies while I checked the gents. Nothing could be as simple as that. Had they left the hotel? I phoned. Nobody had seen them but, yes, they had checked out. Twenty-five minutes to go.

I grabbed a taxi. 'Hotel, step on it!' It was a jungle road, winding, narrow. The tyres screeched their applause each time we rocketed round a bend. Not a sign of them. Another taxi man said he'd had a double ... Back to the airport we tore. I paid double plus fat tip. My expenses would give our company accountant a baby.

The bastards had *already checked through into departure* ...

That should have been it. The usual swollen ankles on the interminable flight to San Francisco. We stayed at the famed Mark

Hopkins hotel, and two of our men had a fist fight in the lobby. I didn't even bother to find out why.

And so back to Heathrow and the baggage carousel where suddenly every last one of them except two just vanished. The two were a pair of gentle sisters who had been tacked on to make up numbers. They had been eternally grateful for everything, no trouble. They looked patient and forlorn.

'Hello, anything wrong?' I asked.

'Oh no,' one said. 'Go on, tell him Dorothy.'

'Well, actually, our bags have been sent to Japan!'

There was a strange feeling of normalcy about it.

Some freebie trips were misdirected; the wrong journals were invited because some nitwit hadn't read the runes. Just prior to the hiatus in the Lebanon a brave attempt was made to promote it as an ideal yachting venue. A marina was built and a worldwide press invitation was sent out. The star attraction was chosen with masterly ineptitude – a Grand Race for an obscure class of dinghy, although until we'd arrived this was not announced.

Two of us opted out: me, because my magazine wasn't even faintly interested in the kicks and jerks of dinghy-boys suspended on wires, and the other because he shouldn't have been invited in the first place, him being a religious correspondent on one of the lesser dailies.

They gave us a cab and a courier for the day and sent us to look at antiquities. A Roman skull peered out coyly from a hole; there were corsair cannonballs and a great many broken bits of masonry. For some reason America was out of favour. Villagers assumed us to be Yanks, and a crowd gathered. 'Rhubarb, rhubarb!' it cried angrily. Our cab was set upon, and things turned nasty. Fists pounded the roof. There were kicks and much spitting at windows, and furious hairy faces scowled at us. Hussain said to Yussuf, 'Let's turn the bastard over!'

It was scary. They had the cab rocking, each rock accelerating, courier moaning, driver praying, us side-by-side, hands in laps looking sick as owls and British. The police car arrived just as the rocking was reaching top-dead-centre.

Lebanese driving was another *divertissement*. Everything must be overtaken. Once, on a narrow road where overtaking was impossible, our driver, howling along at seventy, overtook another car by detouring in and out of a garage forecourt. In our wake we left a haze of burnt rubber and a rocking pump attendant.

Holy Joe, the religious correspondent, was a pale young man and randy as a tinker's ferret. He took a taxi. The driver was pimping for the local tarts. He said, 'Would sir fancy meeting some pretty girls, veery friendly?' Well Joe would, wouldn't he. Then he remembered belatedly who he was and chickened out, quitting the cab and doing a runner. He came banging on my door. 'Hide me, hide me!' He bolted into my room and hid in the loo.

'Serves you bloody right!' I said wrathfully.

He got me to go down on reconnaissance to the lobby. There was a huge, bald, moustachioed thug with a scowl like a folded tent. Behind him stood three old trouts in miniskirts and many beads, ladies of the night and thirsting for blood.

We were due to fly home next morning. Holy Joe moved in with me. Every time room service knocked on the door he shot into the loo. Next morning I had to do my Indian scout act and vet the cab that he boarded at speed with a coat over his head like a prisoner being hustled into the Old Bailey.

I launched a regular feature called The Confessional. Readers were invited to own up to their nautical cock-ups and in turn received a Certificate of Absolution signed by me. As I write, it is still running, over twenty years later. Perhaps it was a recollection of childhood, Saturday nights and the dusty, musty, piety-reeking confines of the confessional, where I mumbled my shame to a despairing Irish priest and received a bargain absolution for the price of an 'Our farter and tree howlie Marys'. I would escape, fully shriven and light of foot. Readers enjoyed the same relief.

I never divulged my own guilty secret. But now I must clear my conscience. *I can't do sums*! It dates to schooldays when I made the transition from a deep turnip-country catholic elementary school, where the standard of maths was based upon the possession of eight fingers and two thumbs, to a big city school which was advanced. The existence of algebra was not even guessed at by me, yet the new school was midway through the second book. The regime of scalding abuse and derision doled out by the teacher resulted in a kind of dyslexia for numbers which still affects me. 'You great stupid fool!' The cry comes echoing down the years.

'Mister Fullerton, *sir*, you are long, long in your box, but you sure as hell fixed me!'

It meant that navigation became a simple, basic folk art for me. The old-time coasting ketch and schooner men used it. A chin-on-forearm gazing at land and water, a hunching at the course made good, a 'feeling' of drift and set, sense of tide and wind and juxtaposition of headland and overfall. In my logbook I sketched the transits, profiles, this cottage gable over that white gate.

My navigation – pilotage really – was seized upon with delight by those readers who were fellow duffers. I was made an Honorary Member of the Institute of Navigators. I felt such a fraud that I later renounced it from sheer guilt.

My modest holiday periods were still too brief to allow me to attempt ocean passages, which was probably just as well. My flat-earth approach would have found me wandering the oceans like some latter-day Flying Dutchman, condemned to voyage into eternity without sighting land. Mariners encountering me would have crossed themselves devoutly, 'Why 'tis the dreaded spectre hisself!'

Today's plethora of electronic whizz-bangs, GPS to say the least, were not to be found. I had Decca and rarely trusted it when the chips were down. I doubt if I would ever have been able to follow the manuals of instruction in any event.

Which was why Joyce and I embarked upon the homeward leg of the Azores-and-Back-Race with a touch of fatalism. Twelve-hundred miles of sea and sky, my new plastic sextant and a pineapple hanging up in a string bag. It was a discouraging prospect; the scope for cock-up was wide. Yet we never had one.

The boat, *Ooslum Bird*, was owned by Andrew Bray. He and Spike did the outward leg on a sunny run, which meant that we had a niggily Force 5 on the nose, a zigging and a zagging that did nothing to assist navigation. Andrew had worked out a special sight form to cover the area and period. I had my little plastic sextant – it was for the taking of sun sights ... *Never did we sight the sun in that whole two weeks.*

We banged to windward in 400-mile tacks, socked by a swinging pineapple, plastic sextant in hand and the loo lid crashing down like the sword of Damocles.

'For God's sake quit moaning!' Joyce said. It was no place for a respectable mud-sailor. 'And another thing,' she added, 'You don't even *attempt* to lift it!'

I got a faint and wavery RDF bearing on Finesterre. Or was it earwax? In navigational terms it was about as much help as a walking frame in a swamp. The wind vane steering gear went up the spout and so did any hope of crossing the finishing line to hysterical cheers and the blowing of trumpets.

We lay hove-to all day long. There was a threaded rod that had to be reconnected. The whole bloody contraption, as the boat corkscrewed around, was munching and snapping. It was like performing dental surgery on an crocodile. Blood streamed. Mine. Levers, weights and hinges thrust and poked. I kept up a non-stop litany of foul language. Joyce held my ankles. If that chomping bastard had severed the rest of me at least she'd have had *them*! But I won.

We did watch-and-watch, six-and-six. We played Travel Scrabble and dodged the pineapple – not what you'd call an exacting routine, but then we were simple folk. One night I had to disengage the vane gear and duck around the stern of a single-hander. I'm a bit ambivalent on the matter: the odds are ordinarily long enough to be worth a gamble but not in a race when forty or so yachts are all sailing the same route. Whoever it was sailed on into the night blissful as a parachutist wearing a bag of laundry.

Later, at dawn, we were on a collision course with a German container ship – no prospect for a yachtsman with a career plan. I disengaged and ducked. Then they saw us and gave me a friendly wave. If they'd hit us there wouldn't have been much evidence. A pineapple?

My dead-reckoning was never more than sixty miles out. The old-timers were sometimes much further adrift after a winter North Atlantic crossing without star sights. In one case the Eddystone light of Plymouth was assumed to be Ushant. Left-hand-down for the open Channel boys. They hit Devon.

I got another nebulous RDF on Round Island off the Scillies, made a grab for The Lizard, then we were home, Falmouth, and the loo lid fell with a final crash. That goddam pineapple was mushy.

There was another passage which took me out of home waters and Gas-house Creek, outside-all to the Med. You can either go inland through the canals, daisy chains and cowpats or you cross Biscay and coast-hop down Spain and Portugal to Gibraltar the way the ancients did: the Phoenicians, the Vikings and suchlike whose navigation included the release of homing captive ravens brought along as an indication of direction. Those birds must have been bloody livid.

The yacht owner was a mean man. We avoided costly marinas where possible and anchored a bit precariously. At sea, with a huge following sea astern as we rode the Portugese Trades south, we had to strap the main boom amidships to prevent the sail chafing the backstay. Our arms and shoulders were racked by the effort of steering; it was too much for the vane gear to cope with. Massive fishing marker flags loomed and surged past which could have dismasted us. 'Mind my topsides!' the owner moaned. We stopped off at Cadiz for fuel. It was a lesson in religious zeal. The fishing community is largely a cooperative. Being devout catholics, fishing on Sunday is unthinkable. Until one minute after midnight. The fishermen wait in the tavernas getting clocked out of their skulls on house red, watching the clock. It was a Sunday when we berthed in Cadiz, and another yachtsman came over and warned us of what would happen. 'Keep the hell clear of the entrance to the dock.' We asked why. 'Wait and watch!' he said.

At one minute to midnight fishermen poured forth. Whooping and cheering they clambered about two waiting coaches and went rocketing down to the dock where they transferred to their boats. Engines crackled into life, lines were cast off, and, four abreast, they raced for the harbour entrance, crews yelling and cheering. Woe betide your visiting yachtsman, pilot book in hand, mid-channel as usual, eyes popping. 'Doris, get your boathook and fender!'

My recollections of that potentially inspirational passage are of Portuguese bureaucracy carried out to a rhythmic thump of rubber stamps, Spanish bureaucracy and a sleepy official who sat in the sunshine awaiting our awakening with smiling patience. And the matter of the free fresh water.

'It's free!' our tightwad owner rejoiced. 'No charge. As much as we can take and FREE!' So we filled every tank, jerrycan, bottle, kettle, basin and bowl. We washed and shampooed, plugged the cockpit drains and washed the sails, scrubbed the decks, topsides and bilges and, finally, we laundered his entire wardrobe, followed by the towels and sheets. It isn't much of a recollection.

22

Two lousy bottles of plonk • Hot-seat from Turkey • Adriatic • Nothing on the clock

People used to ask me when I was planning to go on holiday so that they could choose some other time for their own. They referred to any particularly black cloud as 'Sleighto-cumulus'. The Beaufort Scale should have been revised. 'Force 7–9, Sleightholme at sea, smacks making for harbour, whole trees in motion.'

My holidays usually followed a long spell of hot and settled weather. There would come a final Friday of heat but the shipping forecasts following in succession would speak unctuously of fast-moving lows and large areas of low pressure in the Atlantic. 'Don't *START* that!' Joyce would warn me, reading my sagging jowls.

I would wonder, guiltily, whether she might not prefer a holiday involving poolside loungers and waiter-service. She put up with me – and the howling wind, snatching anchor, windows streaming with frowst and the gas bottle just running out. One morning, having just listened to the weather forecast, I was whingeing away as normal.

'For God's sake man, you're on holiday. *Enjoy yourself!*'

This particular year ran according to the norm. The boat was on the Orwell in Suffolk; we would sail round to Salcombe and see our grandchildren and Michele and John, and maybe take the kids sailing. Grace Darling probably only set out for a gentle row.

The weather broke. We banged and bashed westward, night-stopping, hanging on our anchor, berthing to lie, plunging on our fenders in gale-racked marinas. We reached Salcombe to find the harbour in sou'westerly turmoil and any hope of getting small kids aboard out of the question. John came out and fixed our peevish engine. We started for home via Alderney, Cherbourg, Le Havre and Fécamp.

Fécamp was where the *Douane* had came searching for smuggled women long ago. I should have known better.

In Cherbourg, where long, long ago we'd had that shindig over the 'Healthy Apple Drink' and the fighting clerics, we bought two bottles of duty-free plonk which the *Douane* solemnly sealed in a locker. It was hardly the stuff of a Bacchanalian orgy: no houris would writhe naked to the tune of flute and drum on that little lot.

We ran east and night-stopped on a buoy in Le Havre, and, on the next day we sailed to Fécamp with our 'Q' flag aloft the whole time, requesting clearance. 'Look, we're a healthy ship with TWO bottles of red plonk aboard!' In Fécamp, having entered in the early afternoon, 'Q' flying, we waited to be cleared. Night fell and I took down the flags. I always did. Burgee, ensign, French courtesy flag, all proper. The 'Q' was on the same halyard as the courtesy flag.

Next morning I was up on deck with a fistful of bunting, hoisting away, when the *Douane* arrived. There were two of them in a Citroën Diane, Noddy's car. Had I any dutiable goods aboard? 'Oui Monsieur.' (By God is there no end to this man's talents!) 'Oui Monsieur, deux bouteilles de vin rouge.'

Where was my 'Q' flag then? This nip-nosed, shaggy-assed, ponsed-up pip-squeak wanted to know. I held it up for official inspection. Why was it not up the mast, huh?

I was carted off, with the offending wine in the Diane to HQ, where a man at a desk put me through the mincer and phoned Le Havre. A serious view was taken. 'For God's sake, *keep* the stuff; it's probably crappy wine in any case!' I protested.

Which really offended them. They fined me fifty quid, escorting me to the bank to draw it out, then back to the boat to re-seal the bond locker.

We sailed at once. We spent the night in a sudden foggy blow, dodging around on the Varne Bank to avoid the bellowing procession of great ships thumping up and down. In Ramsgate, bloody Customs and the Harbour Master boarded us in a dead heat with their palms stuck out. The day after we got back to our mooring the weather forecast changed. An area of high pressure from Vladivostok to Peru covered the British Isles and etc.

It had been one of the nastiest 'holidays' we'd ever had. The previous year there had been that business of 'the point of no return', when we were neither halfway there nor halfway back between an impending gale and a potential lee shore.

We had tried to make up for it by going on a freebie charter to

Turkey, where we were struck down with the Turkish trots. On the flight home the hot seat queue for the loo stretched from Istanbul to Heathrow.

Now came the chance of a freebie to the Adriatic in October. There would be mellow, autumn sunshine, ripeness, calm, and the egrets would be migrating. Show me a migrating egret and I'm anybody's.

We paid Joyce's fare and flew to Venice and a vast Italian marina nearby where the German-owned charter boat, a Gib-Sea 31, was berthed. The cruising area was to be south along the Yugoslav coast – in those days (1983) politically trouble free and encouraging tourism. That was the theory.

I should have checked such things as charts and pilots books more carefully; both were in Italian and German. The radio weather station was Italian.

It was one of those pearly-white days of hazy sunshine and a sea of lavender silk, gently undulating, windless, warm and soothing. 'Mmmmm!' we said in chorus. This was more like it. Except for my nagging little worry. Back in the office I had read up on the Adriatic weather prospects for autumn.

'In the Gulf of Venice, in late September,' wrote the author, 'the blue skies and summer heat may give way to cloud, rain etc, as the *notorious climate of the Venetian winter begins to set in!*' There had been a lot more and none of it cheered me. I had kept quiet about it. Having put the boot in he'd gone on about the winds. There was the Bora from the north, and, in case one tried to run for it, there was the dreaded Scirocco from the south. Licking his goddam pencil he had listed trouble spots. We were headed for one.

Our first port of call appeared ahead like an enchanted city in a fairy tale. I only wish it had been. I could have made a magic wish. No prize for guessing what it would have been. Primrose and pink, slender minarets – a tumble of pastel tones with a thicket of masts. I should have made a wish – like wishing we were back home up Peewit Creek.

I found a berth alongside the harbour wall adjacent to the Harbour Office, whence I headed with our passports and papers. An unbuttoned man at a cluttered desk reached out angrily, bang banged with a stamp, rapped out questions, scowled and repeated them louder.

I didn't know what the hell he was on about so I made the usual faces, the lifted eyebrows, puzzled smile and shaken head, clarifying all by saying, clearly, 'English'. He threw my paperwork back with a 'Oh-sod-off!' gesture. Welcome to Yugoslavia.

Back on board again a cop came along the harbour wall, he was strung about with armament like Geronimo. He was only lacking a rocket launcher. He pointed, 'Yugo!' he rapped.

I smirked obsequiously. 'English,' I said, nodding in friendly fashion.

'NO, YOU GO NOW!' he bellowed, taking a fresh grip of his bazooka and banging his bandoliers. We went. There was a floating pontoon. We berthed alongside. We were destined to do so again. The unwelcome attitude of locals towards visitors was general. With a couple of exceptions it was everywhere we went. I wondered if our German flag had a bearing – wartime recollections die hard. But then the Adriatic is the yachting venue for the Germans, Austrians and Swiss. Under Tito's communist regime tourism had scarcely flourished, but he was dead.

We went shopping for provisions, and it was a disaster. There was a supermarket – communist-style – concrete and angle iron, counter assistants like prison guards, ranks of tins sparsely labelled 'beans' or 'cabbage' in Yugoslavian. We bought a selection of what appeared to be boil-in-the-bag meals, which were to turn out to contain grey sausages, hard haricots and chicken giblets awash in a mulch of grey juices. A large, black-draped photo of Tito tricked out in medals presided over all ...

We decided to give ourselves a treat and dine ashore that night. Tito was there again to put the mockers on it. Everything we ordered was 'off'. End of season. What season? we wondered. The waiter had bicycle clips on. 'Pok chop, stewy rice?' he offered, 'trappist cheesy frut? The wine was so powerful that it anaesthetised our taste buds. Then us. We staggered back to the boat and crashed out.

We coasted south in faint airs and sunshine, 'cheesy frut' forgotten. We anchored for the night in the small bay of Dalja where we inflated the dinghy and went exploring. The dinghy would have fitted into a large handbag. A large handbag might have been a better bet. It was vivid blue and yellow. You sat on the bottom and plied little plastic paddles like beating a batter pudding; the motion caused the heads of rower and passenger to bob up and down in succession and jerk back and forth like a clockwork toy.

We met a man and his dog; it growled. I smiled and raised a hand in a 'Hi-ya' gesture. It was probably a forbidden secret salute. He cut us dead.

Not speaking Italian the weather forecast might as well have been the fat stock prices. We needed a forecast badly. The barometer was pitching, a heavy swell was rolling in, and the sunset and lowering clouds looked like a badly bruised bum. All the scene lacked was the Four Horsemen of the Apocalypse. There was nowhere to go, no other shelter. I paid out a lot of anchor chain. We drank our evening snort, ate our vile sausagey-beanie and turned in. The rain fell like a car wash, thunder boomed and banged, and lightning sizzled all around, but that was all. No wind.

And so we cruised on next day under a clear blue sky, over the silky swell to Novigrad where the chairs were on the tables and there was a funny smell. We knew that smell. We had passed through and survived the Home Winemaking Kit era, the airing cupboard vintages that made sock and knicker pong of Sauterne-type. There was a huge bottling plant nearby.

We went into a baker's shop. There where four men and two women inside who all fell silent. They had heavy, hooded eyes and heavy moustaches, the men as well. Give me a wailing-widow for laughs every time, I thought. Joyce did the nod, nod, smile, you-speak-English bit. Nobody did. The bread should have been rubbed down and varnished.

We sat at a street café table. Round came a Lada on two wheels with a man in the back spraying everything, including us, with insecticide. It was probably an old Yugo folk custom.

We met few other yachts, perhaps due to the lateness of the season. (A few years later there would be flotilla sailing from the Dalmatian coastal ports, but the troubles brewing even now would soon stymie that.) Next came the lovely old port of Rovinj. 'Why you come so late?' an Austrian yachtsman, late himself, asked. 'Watch *a bora is coming!*' he added for laughs.

There were islands. I rowed bobbingly ashore for bread and to top up our disgusting supply of grey giblets. A man watched me land with my shopping bag. I held it up, pointed to my mouth then my stomach. 'Fooooood?' I said, enunciating carefully, munching, rolling my eyes, 'Mar-KET?'

'Buggered if I know, mate;' he said, 'I'm only 'ere on a coach trip!' Each day became a bit cloudier and chillier although there was still little wind. We came to the Limski Kanal, anchored at the head of the waters in complete shelter but little else. No matter, we still had some giblets and cheesy-frut. Then a big German yacht anchored nearby and promptly uncoiled and dropped overboard massive plaited copper cables.

'What's that?' Joyce asked, little Miss Muffet, all wide-eyed. I knew bloody well what it was and why, but I hoped I was wrong.

The night was pure Walt Disney. All we needed was the Valkyrie and a big fat man on the tympani. There was an electrical storm that split the world apart, a head-blasting bombardment, lit by rivers of blue fire, forks of it that ripped around us non-stop.

'Actually you seldom hear of yachts being struck!' I told Joyce in a falsetto voice, waiting to be fried. It was time we were heading for home. In the morning we coasted north in a Force 3 drizzle. At least it had a familiar look about it.

We overtook the German yacht, which had a small jib up and four rolls in the main; in view of the paltry breeze that should have given me a clue. She suddenly rounded up, dropped the lot and began motoring for the small port we had abeam at the time.

'Look at that!' I scorned. 'Engine, engine, engine. I don't know!' And neither did I ... but damn soon I would. Joyce glanced astern. 'Look, fog!' she said.

Astern, the horizon had vanished, obliterated by a line of whiteness. Something about it wasn't right. It was *hissing*. Fog doesn't hiss!

'Christ, it's wind!' And I wasn't blaspheming. 'Hang on to the tiller!' There wasn't time. I got the big genoa – our only headsail – down to the deck, but there was no means of lashing it. There wasn't a spare foot of anything in that happy holiday boat. 'Centipedes', those rubber cord hook things that pluck an eyeball out easy as a pickled onion, were the only provision for sail stowing.

The yacht was a Gib-Sea 31, fin keel and spade rudder, a configuration I had always disliked, but now I had to eat crow, which was a change from ricey-cheesy. The wind and rain, driving a banking sea caught us up and hurled us forward. The speed log needle hit the stop at 12 knots and stuck there. I knew that I had to get the sail off her.

The noise was a solid roar. I got my knife out, groped in the locker for fenders and hacked off three lanyards. Helm down and luff up. Total bedlam, beam-on and flat, feet scrabbling. I got the mainsail halfway down. I couldn't even *reach it*. I tried to bear off again on the run, but the rudder had no bite. STARTER BUTTON.

That marvellous engine started at once, and I banged her full ahead. She came off ...

She bore off and ran like a bird, sails half down and threshing, a bow-wave rising abeam like a pair of wings. Surging and rolling and shuddering she ran, that marvellous little boat.

What now though?

We ran north, parallel with the coast we had sailed, slowly, during a whole week. How far? At this speed ... what speed? How long would it be before we ran out of Adriatic? I struggled to concentrate. Say ten-plus-knots. Four hours?

Visibility was a grey circle around us. The seas were like garden walls: that steep, closely packed, crests blowing like smoke. The Adriatic ends in the Bay of Venice and Trieste, shoal water. By now it would be an unbroken wilderness of driving spume. A stranger unable to find the entrances to shelter would drown.

We were both soaked to the skin, shivering; dusk was already stealing in, deepening the gloom of the day. Then would come night, and I knew we would die unless we could find shelter. The charts aboard were useless and the pilot book, which could have led us to some safe haven, was in Italian.

I remembered the big bay that we had crossed when we left Peran. If we could tuck in under the lee of the cliffs? We ran on. I did sums on my fingers. Another half-hour then.

It was time. I set our bows ten degrees to starboard, angling in towards the coasts. Twenty minutes passed. Half an hour.

'There!'

A rain-blackened wall of rock, foam streaming from a wave burst. I felt my scalp rise. I heaved back on the helm and sheered out from it. Trembling, I resumed my dead run. Another ten minutes and I tried it again. This time we saw no cliff. On again. The sea suddenly calmed, and the wind flurried and died a bit. I knew that we had got under the lee of the headland.

We had no echo-sounder. 'People tinker with instruments,' they'd told us, excusing the lack. Dare I risk anchoring? At low speed I poked our bows to the south, towards where cliffs should be. We ran into near-calm. Suddenly a black wall reared and I bore off. Joyce was making tea. She slopped duty-free scotch into the mugs. I had a fishing line and a winch handle sounding the depth. I found no bottom on what must have been twenty fathoms. So forget anchoring. Maybe we could head inland to the head of the bay? The chart didn't go that far.

'What's that place then?' Joyce said, pointing across the bay. It was Peran, of course, but on a dead lee shore. We could see the lights through gathering darkness. We wouldn't last the night. How long could we keep motoring in circles under the sheltering cliff?

We squared up the sails and got out fenders, bent on new lanyards from a coil of light warp. At that late stage we remembered life-jackets. They were a bit Mickey Mouse, but we put them on. 'Right!' I said and bore off in search of shelter.

But there was no shelter.

In the Adriatic you get storm-surge. The sea level builds up. Venice floods. As we drew closer to Peran it had an odd look about it. *The seawall had vanished.* The place was awash. It was too late to turn back. We shot into the outer harbour to find total chaos. Everywhere you looked fishing craft and yachts were plunging and leaping, slamming back on their mooring lines. Street and harbour arc-lights swung and gyrated, throwing a wild pattern of shadows over all. The inner harbour was a mass of small craft grinding each other to splinters. Where could we go?

In mid-harbour we had earlier noticed a heavy structure like a staging, and we had wondered what it was for. We saw now. From it streamed a dozen yachts, singly moored or one astern another. I headed for it. Joyce crouched on our foredeck, coiled line ready to heave. The bastards just waved us off. I circled, begging by gesture. They looked away. Brothers of the Sea.

By the submerged wall, hanging off, lay a large ferry. Surely somebody would take our line. The bastards waved us off!

There was that floating pontoon. It looked like a sea serpent, undulating, wet-gleaming in the crazy lights. Joyce, my poor dear Joyce, had suffered much, but she stinted nothing. She took a flying leap. The pitching yacht and the heaving pontoon made a lethal couple, but she did it. She landed on all-fours, scrabbled, grabbed a turn with her line and hung on.

We hung out every fender and a saloon settee mattress. During the night a drifting yacht came by and ripped off our bow pulpit navigation light; the pontoon broke away from the wall and dragged out into the middle of the harbour, but we survived.

By mid morning there was a hot, flat calm. We didn't care ... we had given up sailing for ever.

When we got home we heard that the weather had been terrible. We never went near our boat for ten days. There was a lot of money wrapped up in her, so we'd better go and check on our assets.

Out aboard we opened her up, aired her, hoisted sails and aired them too. It seemed easier to just let go the mooring than to jink around on the mooring, wind-over-tide. We went slipping down-river ...

Tail Ender

My sailing wasn't all like that: most was placid, and as wholesome as a school dinner. *Ordinary.* Our gas bottle always ran out at breakfast time; from five hundred others the seagulls always chose our coach roof to crap on; I always got the wet seat in the dinghy. The rest was down to Sod's Law. Well, 'Murphy's Law' if you have delicate susceptibilities – and it takes more than a dab of TCP to cure those. It is Sod's Law that gives the public speaker a faulty trouser zip, brings Jehovah's Witnesses banging on the door when you are on the loo, and, if there's a bottle of double malt to be won in the raffle, guess who wins the box of Highland Shortbread that's been doing the rounds since Culloden.

With Sod's Law you can be sure that if you feel strongly enough about something, the *opposite* will happen. I swore that I would never work in an office. I swore fervently that never, NEVER would I become a London commuter, or use a credit card, or eat Heinz Vegetable Salad again, and I vowed that when I retired we would go off cruising for months at a time. Huh!

I haven't worn well, as they say, implying some sort of sock in need of darning. I am not one of those 'wonderful old men' next to whom you sit at club dinners and who make one anecdote last from soup to sweet trolley. Nobody ever says, 'My God, I'd never have guessed he was eighty!' without adding another five. Still, I have my own hair ... even if the nation does own my hips and teeth.

By the time I retired in '84 we had a Rival 32: a little cruiser with a long stride at sea, eager to be gone. We went. Sod and his Law went with us. My hip joints had gone and been replaced years ago, one-by-one, then one-by-one again – four in total. The last came unshipped again almost within days of being shipped, in spite of the 'Meccano knickers' contraption that I was wearing. A second massive anaesthetic so soon after the first blew something in my skull. It cost a ninety quid consultancy fee to be told that nothing could be done, I had permanent vertigo.

So now my left leg is too long, I have the sort of limp that goes with a parrot on your shoulder (unless I walk with one foot in the

182

gutter), and I am permanently giddy. It puts hopping around on foredecks in a windward-going Force five streets ahead of Russian roulette. I never liked going to windward.

I cannot stare at moving water - or grass or crowds - without losing my balance, which gets me out of cocktail parties and Christmas shopping but sets me ashore solid as a letterbox. So, I watch from the clifftop as other men sail by with their wives asking, 'why is it that *other men* always seem able to get marina berths near the ablutions?'

And Joyce, bless her, she rolls a mean bowl and terrorises slug and aphid. She follows me everywhere ... eyeing the carpet. 'What's that you've brought in on your shoe?' she challenges.

Glossary

Abaft: Behind, eg abaft the mast.
All fours: Tied up, moored with four ropes.
All standing: An abrupt stop.
At the run: Without a stop.
Athwart: Across, eg athwart the deck.

Backs: The wind shifts anticlockwise.
Beam: Breadth of a boat.
Bow: The front of the boat.
Brails: Lines that gather a sail like a curtain.
Bring up: To stop, usually at anchor.
Broach: Driven sideways on to the wind/sea.
Bulls eyes: Spherical blocks; rope guides.

Careening: Heeling a moored boat to expose the bottom.
Clinker: A construction method in which planks overlap (usually the hull of a boat).
Close hauled: Heading into the wind with all sail in tight.
Crabbed: Crabbing, a sideways drift.
Crosstree(s): Lateral mast bracing struts.

Dagger board: A lifting keel.
Dipping lug: An almost square sail. The front top edge is passed round the mast when tacking.

Echo sounder: Electronic instrument recording depth of water below the boat.

Fantail: Sloping end of the stern.
Fended off: Pushed away from, eg a fender (which protects the sides of the boat from hard objects) is placed between hull and whatever.
Fo'c'sle: Fore-castle (historic). The fore part of the ship below deck.
Force ten: Wind of storm force ie around 50 knots.
Freeboard: Height of hull above the water.
Fore reach: Forward and sideways drift.

Gaff mainsail: Four-sided as opposed to triangular shaped mainsail.
Gribble: A wood-boring insect harmful to ship's hull.
Grid compass: Course steered is kept between parallel lines.
Gybe: Changing the boat's direction while heading downwind (ie with the wind coming from behind the boat).
Guardrails: A wire rope, safety 'fence' around the deck edge.
Gudgeon: Rudder hinge, eg an eye fitting over a 'pintle' or spike.
Gunn'les: Gun-wales. Upper edge of a boat's sides.

Hard on the wind/closehauled: Heading into the wind (ie when the wind is coming from the front of the boat).
Heading: Direction the boat is sailing in.

Holding ground: Seabed as a hold for an anchor, good, poor, etc.

Hove-to: Forward progress arrested by adjusting the angle of the sails.

Hull: The actual body of the boat excluding mast, superstructure, rig, rudder.

Kedge: A light anchor.

Ketch rig: Two-masted. The smaller 'rear' mast is forward of the rudder.

Knot: Measurement of boat/windspeed.

Lanyard: A short rope/line for a bucket, etc.

Leading marks: Shore features/marks kept in a line to guide the boat into a channel.

Leadline: A marked plumb-line (rope) used to measure the depth of water.

Lee: Downwind side eg lee sheet, lee rail, lee side.

Log: An instrument, electronic or mechanical, recording distance sailed through the water. Ship's record book.

Luff: Forward edge of a sail. To luff: to head a boat directly into the wind so the boat will slow down.

Miss stays: An intended tack (turn) through the wind that only gets half-way.

Mizzen: The aftermost mast and sail.

Moor: To secure a boat to the shore/mooring buoy etc, using lines/ ropes.

Mud berth: A gully on marshland where a boat can be moored.

Neaped: Stranded between a high 'spring' and lesser 'neap' tide.

Nock: The front upper corner of a gaff sail.

Opening up: Holes in a wooden hull caused by drying and shrinkage.

Overfall: Rough water due to fast tidal current usually over rocks.

Parbuckle: One end of a rope is made fast; the other is taken down beneath an object that is cylindrical eg a spar, and up to the crew who raises the object by hauling the line.

Paying off: When a sailing vessel heads off away from where the wind is coming from.

Peak up: Raise the gaff end (upper outer corner) of a gaff sail.

Pinching: Heading a sailing boat too close to the wind thus losing power.

Pluck: A tow.

Port tack boat: The give-way boat when two boats converge to windward.

Pulpit: Bow and stern safety rails.

Raft: Boats moored side-by-side.

Reach: A stretch of sheltered water.

Reaching: Sailing beam to wind ie the wind coming from the side of the boat.

Rig: The part of the boat that supports and includes the sails. A sailing boat is described by her rig eg bermudan-rigged.

Rooster-tail: Plume of water thrown up by a propeller.

Rucking: Rumpling, creasing eg 'the nock' or mast/gaff corner of the sail.

Scandalise: Reduce the drive of a gaff sail by raising/dropping corners.

Sea-anchor: A canvas 'drag' to hold a ship facing the seas.

Sheered off: Moved away in a lateral direction.

Sheerline: The upward curve of a ship's deck and rail.

Shoaling water: Shallowing water.

Shroud: One of a set of mast-supporting stays.

Solent tides: A second (slightly lower) high tide an hour later.

Soundings: Reference to charted depths of water.

Spring: A mooring rope spanning the whole length of the vessel.

Spring tides/springs: Tides that occur at or near the time when the moon is full and new. High tides are higher than at other times ie neaps and low tides are lower. Current are stronger.

Stays: Supports for the mast. In stays: Head-to-wind (so not moving) and without steerage way

Stern: The back of the boat.

Stopped up: Breaking-stops. Sail stowed thus for quick/easy setting.

Stud-link: Anchor chain link with cross-bar to give strength.

Swim-headed: A barge lighter with blunt, overhanging ends.

Swatchways: East Anglian term. A narrow channel between sandbanks.

Sway aboard: To haul something up and swing it on board.

Tacking: Sailing to windward (ie towards the wind) in a series of zig-zag headings because it is impossible to sail directly into the wind.

Thwarts: Boat seats.

Tide-wind: Becalmed boat. Breeze caused as moved by tidal current.

Tingles: Exterior/interior patches applied to hull planking.

Topping lift: Rope for lifting the end of the boom.

Two-blocks: Said when a tackle is fully tightened, blocks together.

Under-foot: Anchor dropped straight down to act as a drag.

Veer: Clockwise windshift. Let out more anchor cable.

Watch-and-watch: Two crew taking equal and ongoing shifts while the other one sleeps.

Weather window: Brief fine spell in continuous bad weather.

Windward (go to): Driving a boat upwind ie towards where the wind is coming from, beating, tacking.

Wrinkle the nock: Hoist the gaff until creases appear in the sail.